A NEPALESE JOURNEY

A NEPALESE JOURNEY

THE ESSENCE OF THE ANNAPURNA CIRCUIT

ANDREW STEVENSON

THE MOUNTAINEERS BOOKS

Published in North America by
The Mountaineers Books
1001 SW Klickitat Way, Suite 201
Seattle, WA 98134
www.mountaineersbooks.org

First published in North America in 2002 by The Mountaineers Books
First published in the UK in 2002 by Constable & Robinson Ltd.

Edited and designed by Blackingstone Books Limited
Printed in China

Library of Congress Cataloging-in-Publication Data
A catalog record for this book is available at the Library of Congress.

Photographic text captions are based on material taken from
Annapurna Circuit: Himalayan Journey by Andrew Stevenson

ISBN 0-89886-789-4 (NA)

Front jacket: Elderly woman selling trinkets, Muktinath

Back jacket: Chorten on high route between Ngwal and Braga

Half title page: Woman carrying doko in Kathmandu Valley

Title page: Walking down the Kali Gandaki Valley between Kalopani and Larjung, the
deepest valley in the world

Right: Girl ringing bell in main Durbar Square, Bhaktapur

Pages 8–9: Girl with cow, Kathmandu Valley

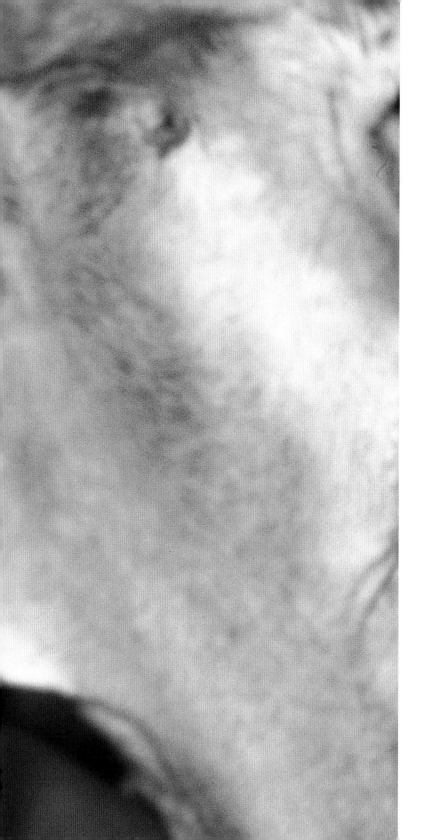

CONTENTS

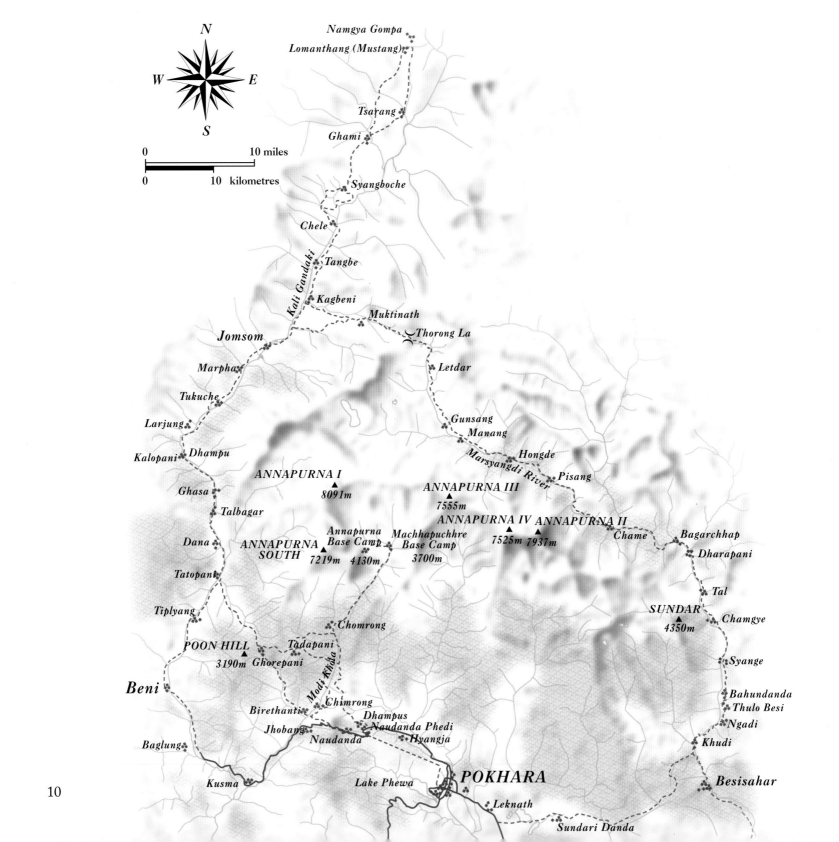

INTRODUCTION

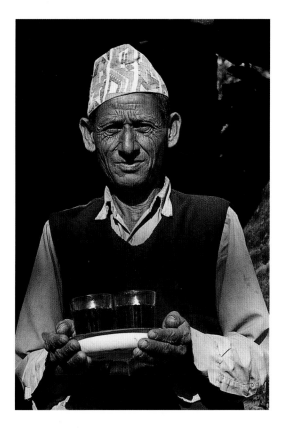

I could have fallen in love with the girl sitting next to me on the Aeroflot flight out of Kathmandu. She had tousled sandy-coloured hair, dirt under her fingernails, and layers of grime behind her ears. She was all of five years old and her mother sat on the other side of her, by the window. I was still on a high and feeling slightly heroic after completing the Annapurna Circuit.

"So, did you go trekking?" I made conversation with Gentiane as her mother watched the serrated saw-blade of the Himalayas slip past the wingtip of the old Turpolov jet.

"Yes," she replied.

"And where did you go?" I asked in that slightly patronizing voice adults reserve for when they talk to children.

"The Annapurna Circuit," she replied, matter-of-fact.

This classic 200-km/125-mile long-distance trekking route ascends the lush, sub-tropical foothills of Nepal along an ancient trading route through the Annapurna Himal, crosses the frozen, windswept Thorong Pass into the desert landscape of the hidden Kingdom of Mustang, descends the deepest gorge in the world, with 8,000-m/5-mile high mountain peaks looming on either side, back to tranquil Lake Phewa. If the most arduous of holidays are those best remembered, then the Annapurna Circuit is an experience that will undoubtedly remain indelibly etched in one's psyche.

Two years ago, in late May, I broke my back in an accident, shattering the L-2 vertebra. As I lay in hospital immobilized within two back braces and a hallucinogenic haze brought on by five days of morphine, I promised myself I would get back on my feet in time to walk the Annapurna Circuit before the end of the trekking season. It was perhaps an unrealistic goal, but it was a vision that buoyed my spirits those first two depressing weeks, and then kept me pushing the barriers of pain in the succeeding months of recuperation as I began a self-imposed regimen of swimming and then walking and finally jogging. In the event, I didn't go back to the Annapurnas. Instead, I walked up to Everest Base Camp, that December.

Tea stall on the route between Kathmandu and Dumre

Although I have returned to different areas of Nepal a dozen times, I seem to have reserved walking around the Annapurnas for those watershed periods in my life when I have the most to contemplate. In so many ways, the Annapurnas have become a personal touchstone for me, and the Annapurna Circuit in particular has an appeal that reaches somewhere deep within my soul, as if this is a part of the world where I belong. Perhaps that romantic notion is not so outrageous. This is, after all, a rugged realm of reincarnation, its intrinsic spirituality celebrated within the monasteries overlooking each village, and symbolized by the numerous stone prayer walls and chortens lining the paths, and the innumerable prayer flags fluttering from every exposed ridge or pass.

Before tackling the Annapurna Circuit for the first time, I had travelled to Nepal on five previous occasions as a development economist, evaluating Canadian-funded aid projects in isolated, often restricted, areas of the country. I have visited most of Nepal including, most recently, Upper Mustang, and the Annapurnas remain without a doubt my favourite area; I would happily hike the Circuit every year, discovering more about its people, the mountains, and myself. It's as much an addiction for this meditative stroll with a heavy backpack as the spiritual insights stimulated by the spectacular Himalayan scenery, and the lessons to be learned from the simplicity, generosity and humour of its mountain people.

Findings in graves contained within caves high in cliff faces indicate that the Marysangdi and Kali Gandaki Valleys, cutting through the otherwise impenetrable Himalayas, have served as vital trade routes between the plains of India and Tibet and Central Asia for at least 3,000 years. Communities surviving in this inhospitable and increasingly fragile environment have always had to rely on a precarious living based on agriculture and pastoralism, supplemented to varying degrees of success, dependant on the prevailing hegemony and strategic allegiances of the day, on trade. This easily malevolent land of frozen winds and earthquakes, of mudslides and avalanches, disease and drought, has fostered a healthy respect for the supernatural. The inhabitants, seeking tangible links to a natural

Lake Phewa, Pokhara, looking north at the Annapurnas

world beyond their control and haunted by spirits and demons, have marked their realm with reassuring corporeal edifices: piles of stones, temples, walls and portals. Their significant entreaties to appease are further evidenced in the prayer flags, prayer walls, and prayer wheels found in their villages and on every auspicious pass or ridge.

While the geological obstacles are formidable enough, it's the modern political barriers that have made the Annapurna Circuit unique. Unlike the rest of the Nepalese Himalayas, the Annapurna mountain range does not form the border between Nepal and Tibet. Since 1977, when Manang and Lower Mustang on the north side of the Himalayas were no longer confined as restricted districts, one can hike through the Annapurna Himalayas to the Tibetan Plateau on the other side, to what is essentially, both geographically and ethnically, Tibet. Given the Chinese occupation of that country, only a short distance away, it is perhaps a more authentic insight into a vanishing Tibetan way of life than exists in Tibet itself. Making this area of the Himalayas even more alluring is the possibility of doing a circuitous route, up the Marsyangdi River to Manang, over the 5,416-m/17,769-ft Thorong Pass into Mustang, and down an entirely different river system, the Kali Gandaki, back to Pokhara.

What was an adventure a couple of decades ago, a logistical challenge involving a trekking expedition carrying tents and stores of food and a retinue of staff, is done increasingly easily on one's own with the minimum of equipment, staying at the numerous bhattis or teahouses straddling these historic trade routes.

I recall in the hot pools in Tatopani an ex-hippy turned corporate lawyer describing in disgruntled terms how wonderful Nepal used to be in the 1970s and how it had gone downhill ever since. I remember thinking how wonderful Nepal was now, and how wretched this foreign visitor seemed, living in the past. Having seen the changes that have taken place over the last fifteen years, I

Left: En route from Chame to Bhratang, looking west

Right: Carrying dokos full of pine needles for barns in Upper Pisang, Pisang below, with Annapurna II behind

too have to be wary of casting aspersions. Change, the Buddha admonished, is a part of life; the easier we accept these changes, the happier we will be.

The purist may lament the transformation that has taken place in the Annapurnas as a result of tourism, but many of these developments are inevitable and perhaps even welcome, making the trip less hazardous for the visitor and raising the standard of living of the local people by providing a constant source of income for villagers who had few opportunities for livelihood beyond subsistence agriculture at poverty level. Villages that were once dying are being infused with the talents of their younger people who are returning to their birthplaces to make a living from the increasing numbers of tourists passing through.

Because of its growing popularity, what was once a short trekking season of October–November and March–April now extends from the end of the monsoons in September right through the winter into May. Hiking recently to Upper Mustang in early March, there were plenty of trekkers crossing the Thorong Pass from Manang to Mustang, despite the snow. The increasing numbers of lodges have not only extended the seasons, but are also opening up side valleys and alternative routes.

An additional appeal to the Annapurnas is their easy access. Herzog's epic climb up Annapurna I in June 1950 took months of walking just to get to Tukuche on the Kali Gandaki, now a hop-skip-and-jump away from Jomsom, itself a twenty-five-minute flight from Pokhara. Poon Hill, Annapurna Base Camp and even Jomsom and Muktinath are relatively easy goals, within a matter of several days of Lakeside.

The one route that hasn't been trivialized is the Annapurna Circuit itself. Local buses carrying independent trekkers leave from Kathmandu, turn directly north at Dumre, on the main road to Pokhara, and continue along the dirt track, now black-topped, to the trailhead at Besisahar, cutting at least two days off the start of this classic walk. At the other end of the Circuit, the Chinese-built road snakes its way westwards and northwards from Pokhara all the way to Beni on the Kali Gandaki. This reduces the tail end of the Annapurna Circuit by another three or four days, circumvents the long climb up to Ghorepani, the knee-crunching descent to Birethanti, and the subsequent walk along the ridgeline overlooking Lake Phewa to Pokhara. The Circuit once took a good twenty-one days to complete; with the roads reaching further north at Besisahar and Beni it can now be completed in almost a fortnight.

Despite the recent infrastructure, the walk up the Marsyangdi Khola and the hard slog over the Thorong Pass remain daunting prospects, matched by one's sense of achievement when contemplating the trip afterwards from the comfort of a Lakeside restaurant. Every time I see the Annapurna Himalayas from Pokhara I am amazed that I circumnavigated those immense mountains on my own two little feet.

Historically, villagers in the Annapurnas lived by traditional laws that successfully preserved their flora and fauna. Subsequent to the Nepalese central government nationalizing all forests in the 1950s, local villagers ceased their long-established methods of conservation, no longer viewing the fauna and flora as their own, but as the government's, to be plundered at will. Villagers no longer cared and the chopping down of trees, and the hunting of wild animals, accelerated at an alarming pace. The problem was so grave a landmark decision was made when the central government created the Annapurna Conservation Area and, in a unique experiment at the time, returned responsibility for the forests back to the local communities.

When the idea was first raised of making the Annapurnas a conservation area, rather than relocating its inhabitants (as had been done before in other areas of Nepal, like Rara Lake), the needs of the local people were integrated into the concept of preserving the area. Unlike the original American model of national parks, the Annapurna Conservation Area was to include the indigenous population in a multi-use area so that jurisdiction and ownership of their immediate environment was vested once again in the local people. While it was easy enough to break the law when a police

Spinning the wheels of a prayer wall, Upper Pisang

officer from another region, speaking a different dialect, attempted to monitor an area from a neighbouring village, it is difficult or impossible to poach an animal or chop down a live tree without someone in the same community knowing.

The Annapurna Conservation Area Project (ACAP), a Nepalese project under the King Mahendra Trust for Nature Conservation, was established in 1986 to help manage the designated conservation area with the active participation of local people. By handing accountability of their natural resources back to the local villagers, a sense of collective responsibility has returned, particularly in areas where ACAP has worked the longest: the pilot areas, including Ghandrung, Ghorepani and Chomrong. In these relatively homogenous Gurung villages, ACAP's programme to sensitize the local population to the need to conserve their environment and fauna has had dramatic results. Combined with solar heating, fuel-efficient ovens, micro hydro-powered electricity, proper management of harvesting new wood, and assistance in providing subsidized kerosene supplies, the forests and fauna are regenerating.

Economic development cannot be separated from environmental sustainability. The enormous problem of deforestation was exacerbated by the vast quantities of timber used in the construction of lodges, and supplying the kindling required for cooking and hot water, demanded by ever-increasing waves of trekkers. Areas like Ghorepani were being visibly stripped of their rhododendron forests.

There is room for optimism, however, and the situation has been ameliorated through promoting simple technologies, and educating trekkers and locals alike. Solar-heated showers in conjunction with "back-boilers" (pipes running through insulated cooking ovens connected to an adjacent barrel of water) augment the supply of hot water without increasing the fuel consumption of the wood-fired stoves. The insulated enclosed stoves themselves are far more fuel-efficient than their open-sided, smoky predecessors. Where there is electricity, electric cookers can be used for boiling rice. On the other side of the equation, trekkers are advised to order meals ahead of time so that they can be prepared simultaneously,

Kitchen, Red House Lodge, Kagbeni

and to avoid lodges not using fuel-saving techniques. In many areas, notably the Annapurna Sanctuary, wood fires are forbidden, and kerosene stoves must be used for cooking.

These efforts to implement fuel-saving techniques are first made in the teahouses and lodges catering to tourists. From their examples the effect has spread, slowly, to more traditional homes and villages. But as deforestation in certain regions looks to be declining, in other districts the problem is getting worse. The Annapurnas comprise a huge area and a bewilderingly diverse ethnic population base. Although the Gurungs, farmers and shepherds of the middle hills (famous for their dominant role as Gurkha soldiers in the British army) make up the majority of the population of the Annapurnas, there is a profusion of other indigenous tribes, as well as a baffling hierarchy of castes, including Brahmins (the Hindu priest caste) and Chhetris (the Hindu warrior caste), and an increasing influx of Tibetan refugees settling in the upper reaches of the Annapurnas.

I remember coming across a line of thirty of so men, women and children descending the path. One look and it was obvious that these were traumatized Tibetan refugees. The abject expression on all their faces, even the children, reflected their exhaustion and shock. They resembled battle-weary veterans, as if they had been through and survived a war – which they had. It was heart rending to witness these exiles so soon after they had made an arduous escape over difficult high passes to flee their occupied country. I can't forget those distressed faces, or their haunted eyes. Two unarmed Nepalese policemen escorted this sad, silent procession, probably to a Tibetan refugee camp where, depending on the politics of the day, they would either be permitted to stay, or handed back to the Chinese.

There is a saying in Nepal that trekkers come to the country for the mountains, but return because of the people. There is, without a doubt, a kaleidoscope of folk to befriend in the Annapurnas. The Manangi from Manang, and the Loba from the Kingdom of Lo, inhabit the regions north of the Himals, although there are sub-groups within these two. There are plenty of Khampas, refugees from the province of Kham in Tibet, many of

20

whom were trained by the CIA to make incursions into Chinese-occupied Tibet, either living amongst the other tribes in their villages or occupying their own villages. The Baragaunle, the people of "twelve villages", occupy the upper Kali Gandaki, including Kagbeni and Muktinath. The Thakalis controlled the old trade route lower down along the Thak Khola stretch of the Kali Gandaki, but even they are divided into a multiplicity of clans. The Gurungs farm the higher middle hills, although many of the other Mongolian-featured ethnic groups further north and higher up will also call themselves Gurung; the Magars, Rai, Limbu and Tamangs work the middle and lower hills, and are also recruited as stalwart Gurkha soldier material. The Newars, normally found in the Kathmandu Valley, fill occasional pockets, their villages easily identified by the elaborate woodwork on window frames and doors. Often there are Dolpo to be seen on the trail, herding yak down from the high summer pastures to be butchered for meat before the winter, or sadhus from India making the pilgrimage to Muktinath. Many Sherpas from the Solu Khumbu (Everest region) may be encountered too, working for trekkers as guides or sidhars (leaders). There are no hard-and-fast rules as to who lives where, and often more than one tribe may inhabit the same village, professing to be both Hindu and Buddhist, or maybe even blending in a dash of animism, depending on their location and the pervasive influences that have swept through their villages over hundreds, even thousands, of years.

While Nepal is 90 per cent Hindu and His Majesty's government has decreed that the Hindu caste system is to be abolished, these proclamations do not reflect the dramatic changes already taking place as a result of tourism. The traditional caste system is breaking down, to be replaced by a hierarchy measured by material wealth where one's caste, even as an untouchable, is rendered meaningless, at least in this incarnation. In the Annapurnas, Brahmins or Chhetris, the highest Hindu cultural castes, are more likely to work as labourers in the lodge of a Buddhist Gurung family than vice versa.

Outside Ngwal, looking west, Annapurnas to the south

Tourism is a means by which a villager can extricate himself out of an otherwise vicious cycle of poverty and as a result the competition amongst teahouse owners for the trekking business is cut-throat. It was pitiable to witness trekkers bargaining for the price of a bed, or a meal. Often lodging was offered free if the trekkers would only eat there, an ineffective loss leader if a trekker sleeps in one lodge and eats in another. ACAP has empowered teahouse owners by standardizing menus and fixing minimum prices for meals and lodging. Some lodges may charge more for fancier facilities and more exotic meals, but there is a minimum level too that protects the smaller teahouses.

Every visitor to the Annapurnas pays an entrance fee to ACAP. Quite different from other aid-dependent recipients, ACAP has the opportunity to become self-sufficient and sustainable, relying on continued revenue derived directly from tourism. ACAP's programmes include forest management, provision of alternative energy resources, community development, trail and bridge maintenance, health and education projects, tourism management training, agriculture and agroforestry, cultural heritage conservation, and promoting women in development.

On these well-travelled routes, the trekking groups with their entourage of staff and supplies of food, tents, and furniture have become redundant. It was estimated that less than 10 per cent of what clients paid for these expeditions filtered into the local economy. The extensive network of teahouses has removed the need for an entourage of porters, guides, sidars, cooks and porters carrying tents and mattresses, tables and chairs, pots and pans. To pay 100 dollars to sleep in a tent seems ridiculous when as little as 10 dollars a day would suffice to sleep and eat well in a more comfortable teahouse. Although teahouse owners must buy some food supplies from outside their community, the majority of trekkers now using local facilities means that most of their expenditure goes directly into the local economy, not the trekking outfit in Europe or America, or their sub-agents in Kathmandu. Nevertheless, trekking outfitters still play an important role in exploring new areas, such as in the

Hermitage, Manang

22

Siklis area of the Annapurnas, where their pioneering efforts will eventually pave the way for the establishment of a chain of enterprising villagers opening local teahouses.

The result of the annual tourist money flowing into the trekking corridors is readily apparent, and the economic benefit spills over to neighbouring villages and valleys too. Not all teahouse owners can grow their own food, so villagers off the beaten trail supply them with fresh vegetables, fruit, or even wood. Aside from the questions of ecology, this is sustainable economic development in the sense that, unlike aid projects or local non-governmental organizations (NGOs) that are financed with foreign aid money and are therefore dependent on the donor's whim for continued funding, income from tourism can continue indefinitely as long as the area remains attractive to visitors. Most communities along the Annapurna Circuit have access to clean drinking water, schools, health clinics and even electricity, often paid for directly through the wealth that tourism has created, or indirectly through ACAP assistance.

Figures for the numbers of trekkers visiting the Annapurnas, despite overall figures for Nepal dropping off, have increased to 70,000, providing ACAP with over 2 million dollars in annual funding, and it is becoming increasingly important for the project to reach out to its constituents to reinforce the links between tourism and the environment, and the income available to fund its numerous development projects.

As might be expected, economic and environmental problems differ from district to district. ACAP's ambitious programme extending from the original Gurung populations around Ghandrung, to the Manangi of Manang and the Loba of Lo in Upper Mustang, has created the inevitable challenges that beset any development agency. Complexities in local and national politics and competing aid agencies compound these problems. ACAP itself has expanded, from a handful of members in a dedicated team working at grassroots level with a base in Ghandrung to a fully-fledged bureaucracy with hundreds of employees, many of whom are based

Left: Older woman en route from Bahundanda to Syange
Right: One of the few young children left in Upper Pisang

out of ACAP's headquarters in Pokhara. Nowadays the community of Gurungs around the Ghandrung area feel they are skilful enough to handle their own development projects without the interference or administrative costs of ACAP. The relatively well-off Thakalis along the Kali Gandaki, with their well-honed, centuries-old tradition of providing accommodation to traders, may always have thought ACAP management courses on tourism were redundant anyway. The Manangi, on the other hand, are enterprising individualists, often well travelled internationally but not necessarily used to working together with other Nepalese communities. In Mustang the inhabitants are desperately poor, have high expectations of what ACAP can do for them, and want more of a share of the income generated from tourism. While tourists are often most concerned about environmental issues, and the quality of the pathways and bridges, food and lodging, the inhabitants of the Annapurnas are more interested in income, education and health care facilities. Somehow ACAP has to keep all these disparate interests mutually inclusive rather than exclusive.

Over the years, working in the development field in Africa and Asia, one of the basic misconceptions I heard expressed by Westerners is that poverty in the Third World is simply a result of overpopulation and high population growth. In Nepal, as in the Western world some generations ago, children are considered an asset; they contribute to the economic viability of the household, assisting in the harvest and daily chores. They provide security in their parents' old age or ill health. The death rate of Nepalese children under five years old is amongst the highest in the world. There is, in other words, every reason for the Nepalese to have as many children as possible.

Now, in many households along the trekking routes in the Annapurnas, parents are having only two children because they have reached a certain critical economic threshold where they feel secure enough to look after themselves in old age, or ill health, and perhaps more importantly are investing in their children's education. Instead of contributing to the mundane tasks involved in a subsistence farm, their children are attending school and therefore costing money. In some cases they attend private boarding schools

in Pokhara or Kathmandu. Tourism is helping these communities break out of their chronic cycle of poverty. Whether those children raised in Kathmandu or Pokhara will return to their home villages is another question; if they don't, their places in the lodge will be taken by other less fortunate children, often orphans.

With the trade between Nepal and Tibet – traditionally Tibetan rock salt in exchange for rice from the foothills – severely curtailed by the Chinese occupation of Tibet, the off-season employment opportunities for the armies of porters and muleteers would be virtually non-existent were it not for the tourist business and the constant demand for supplies from lodges, even during the off-season. Many of the porters and guides are farmers and work in the tourism sector to supplement their income from marginal smallholdings that are unable to support their families. Employment in the services of a trekker may be essential to their survival.

This leads to a moral conundrum of sorts: is it better to hire a porter, or even a guide, or go with a trekking outfit, or is it feasible to set out on one's own?

I prefer to travel alone. It's a chance to discover something about myself, to learn, to meet people and make new friends, without restriction. Admittedly, as a male, I am less likely to be harassed and there are areas, in dense forests nearer the trailheads, where it is advisable to walk with others. But it's more likely that one will meet someone compatible on the trail rather than by posting a notice outside a hotel in Kathmandu, or being stuck for the duration with members on a group trek. Many other individual travellers start out on the trail on exactly the same footing, a little insecure, looking for friends.

There is no necessity for a "guide" to get around the Annapurnas. There is a profusion of sufficiently accurate maps, several detailed guidebooks, and ample people on the trail to ask directions. A suitable Nepalese guide from the area can certainly enrich the experience. Too often, though, guides are not from the Annapurna region, inexperienced, and moonlighting during the trekking season. There are many excellent guides reflecting the

characteristics of the Nepalese – friendly, humorous, fun loving, honest, easy-going and yet hard working – and these positive qualities undoubtedly describe the majority. Unfortunately there are also stories of clients, particularly single women, who have had to dismiss their guides, even when, or perhaps especially when, their services for the entire trip have already been paid for. A guide can make or break your trip. A guide*book*, on the other hand, doesn't have such a pervasive influence, especially if it's sitting at the bottom of your pack.

Taking a porter or not depends on whether you want to carry your own pack. While someone calling himself a "guide" will not generally do that for you, a porter is often knowledgable enough to act as a guide. Probably the biggest difference between someone describing himself as a guide, or a porter, is his ability to speak English. On our trip to Lomanthang we had a "guide" who had never been in Upper Mustang before and was therefore totally ineffective at providing any insights into the area. Generally speaking, a "guide" in Nepal is understood to mean someone who can speak English and show you the route, but who will not necessarily, especially if he isn't from the region, have any more understanding of the area than you can read about in the ubiquitous guidebooks.

Whatever one decides to do there is a mutual responsibility between client and guide/porter. The relationship can be successful, but there are times too when it doesn't work. On the other hand, if one does set out too ambitiously on one's own, there is still every chance of finding a porter from a village on the trail. I once carried a pack that weighed 32 kilos/70½ lb. Hardly surprisingly, within three days my left knee became badly inflamed and I had to hire a local porter returning to his home higher up the valley. I couldn't have asked for a better companion, and because he was a local he knew the area intimately. I stayed at his home, met his family, and the two of us were genuinely sorry when we parted.

For those trekkers who have a tendency to feel guilt-ridden for carrying their own packs and not distributing their wealth, it's easy

Meditating Nepalese sadhu

27

enough to find a headmaster at a local school who will be more than willing to relieve trekkers of their remorse and donations.

Trekking on your own or with a friend, carrying your own pack, you make your own decisions on how far to go, where to eat and sleep, and therefore escape succumbing to a guide's often different agenda. A guide's choice of lodge may have more to do with how much baksheesh he makes from the owner than the quality of the accommodation or food. On your own, you have the freedom to choose to do as you want. Some days you may feel energetic and walk for several hours; at other times you might walk for half an hour, meet some friendly locals, have a cup of tea, and get no further. Sometimes you might feel like meeting other Westerners, at other times you might want to be by yourself. Walking around the Annapurnas is like holding a dinner party without having to either prepare the meal or invite the guests or, for that matter, stay up for the evening. There are few opportunities back home to meet people with such a wide range of backgrounds, professions and nationalities. Evening meals with other foreign trekkers in a bhatti can be a fascinating experience in its own right. Having met interesting fellow trekkers one might continue walking with them for some days; if not, you can walk slower or get up later, and encounter another wave of trekkers. Walking in the Himalayas is a time to ruminate, meditate, ponder life's great questions, or, more often than not, an opportunity to empty one's head of ruminations, meditations, and the endless pondering over life's great questions!

Although meeting others is an added dimension, it is easy to deliberately get out of "sync" with the majority of trekkers staying at the same popular villages or lodges. A village recommended by the guidebooks may have every bed occupied, and yet a village or teahouse half an hour before or after will be empty. The many excellent guidebooks on walking in the Annapurnas are well worth reading, but they should not be used as an alternative to using one's own initiative. Sadly, some bhattis, and even whole villages, are bypassed because the guidebooks do not include them.

To reduce the frequency of encounters with other trekkers, try hiking in the shoulder seasons, setting out in late November to December when most trekkers have made tracks for home. More and more visitors are trekking through the winter months; although the temperatures are colder and there is risk of snow, the weather is stable and consistently clear and often you might find yourself the only person in a bhatti or village.

My suggestion to walk independently is not to belittle the trekking outfitters. They pioneer new routes and take guests into places that are less frequented, without the infrastructure of local bhattis. In the Annapurnas, organized trekking expeditions are still exploring new trails, including the Siklis area. Travelling around these regions on your own without tents and staff would certainly be possible, definitely rewarding, but not as easy, and probably more time-consuming. On the other hand, the fact that trekking permits from the central government are no longer necessary means the intrepid visitor has more freedom to hike almost wherever he wants, except in semi-restricted zones.

With the two roads encroaching at the beginning and end of the Circuit, it is easier to complete the trip well within the three weeks usually suggested for this epic walk. There are those who complete the Circuit in two weeks or less, and I remember one person bragging that he had "done" it in eleven days. But the point is not to walk the Circuit in as little time as possible, shunning the best parts of the route and therefore diminishing the experience. If you've got the time, take the extra effort required to climb up to the "high route" stretching from Upper Pisang through Ghyaru and Ngwal to Braga. This stretch of the trail is without a doubt the highlight of any part of the Annapurnas, and yet it seems to be overlooked by many trekkers who make a beeline from Pisang to Manang, along the valley bottom. It is worth taking the extra time, if one has it, to climb the high route, explore the Khangsar Valley, ascend to Ice Lake above Braga, or visit the lama in the hermitage above Manang. And don't be tempted to take the shortcut from Muktinath/Jharkot to Jomsom, cutting out Kagbeni, the most authentic walled village in Mustang open to foreigners without

Khangsar Valley, looking west towards Tilicho Lake, Annapurnas to the south

paying the substantially higher fees to go into Upper Mustang. A few days spent in Kagbeni can be a worthwhile insight into the harsh life in this remote corner of the world.

The point should be not to see how quickly one can do these walks so much as how much time one can devote to savour the incredible diversity of cultures, geography, flora and fauna, geology, religions, ethnic types and architecture.

During my time trekking in the Annapurnas many of the owners of lodges have become friends. I'm often amazed at how much attention they will devote to one wayward but communicative traveller despite the multitudes they must see passing through, and I am constantly impressed by the generosity of villagers encountered en route. It is surprisingly easy to scratch beneath the surface to share in their lives, simply by not rushing.

I've been fortunate enough to have lived and travelled in many beautiful corners of the world; they all have their intrinsic attributes. But a long meditative walk in the Annapurnas is still a place I fantasize of returning to. All I have to do to conjure those dreams is open a map of the Annapurnas and imagine myself following the flagstone pathways between lofty peaks, through familiar villages, and once again I can feel the tugging at my heartstrings as I am transported back to that magical land.

I trust these images capture the essence of your own walk in the Annapurnas, and convey the experiences of hiking amongst these spectacular mountains and the special people who make it their home. For those still contemplating this trek, I hope these photos are inspirational in taking those first steps to making your dreams come true.

The Kali Gandaki, looking north, between Kagbeni and Chele, Upper Mustang

POON HILL

to page 68

Phalante

Chitre

Deurali

Tadapani

Kimror

POON HILL ▲ Ghorepani Banthanti

3190m

Banthati

Ulleri

Syauti Baz

Tirkhedhunga

Hille

Sudame

Birethant

Pokhara, meaning touristic Lakeside, still exudes that sleepy, slightly dishevelled atmosphere it inherited from the days when hippies hung out here. Somehow, probably because of its proximity to beautiful Lake Phewa, Pokhara doesn't convey the same sense of congestion and frenetic activity experienced in Kathmandu. Arriving in Pokhara is a welcome relief from the noise and pollution of Nepal's capital.

Despite its lingering charm, reinforced concrete hotels several storeys high are thrown up every year, sprawling luxury resorts increasingly dot the valley, and a sealed road along the lake replaces what was once just a dusty track. Restaurants and bookstores, supermarkets and souvenir shops, illegally line the lake-side of the road; hotels and restaurants have proliferated over to the other side of the lake, still accessible only by boat.

Continued unrestricted development will ultimately turn Lake Phewa and Lakeside into an urban sprawl. The most expensive and exclusive resorts are already enclaves: havens built out of paddy fields in the Pokhara Valley, removed from the busy, dusty town and its beautiful lake. But the wooden boats powered by paddle or sail, the water buffalo grazing lazily on the grassy banks, and the spectacular view of the Annapurnas early in the morning, remain prevailing impressions of Lakeside's bucolic origins.

Pokhara is the "base camp" for most excursions into the Annapurnas. When I first walked the loop to Ghorepani and Poon Hill, I climbed up to Sarankot and then followed the ridge overlooking the lake to Naudanda where I stayed for the night, before continuing to Chandrakot. Now it is possible to spend the night in the relative luxury of Pokhara and early the next morning take a taxi on a road to the top of Sarankot to witness the sunrise.

Access into the mountains has been facilitated by the Chinese-built road which extends from Pokhara, crosses through Naudanda, descends west to cross the Modi Khola (the river that drains the Annapurna Sanctuary) at Naya Pul, and then descends along the Modi Khola to ascend up the Kali Gandaki to Baglung and Beni. Whether this road will continue further north to Lomanthang in Upper Mustang, where a dirt road already extends down from the Tibetan border, is a mute question.

When I was working as a development economist, I remember travelling to countries in Africa and Asia doing base-line surveys, asking villagers what they wanted most. It's a fairly typical story all over the world. Road access is often one of the perceived necessities for development, giving easier access to markets and hospitals. More recently I asked villagers around Naudanda what they thought now of the road that passes through

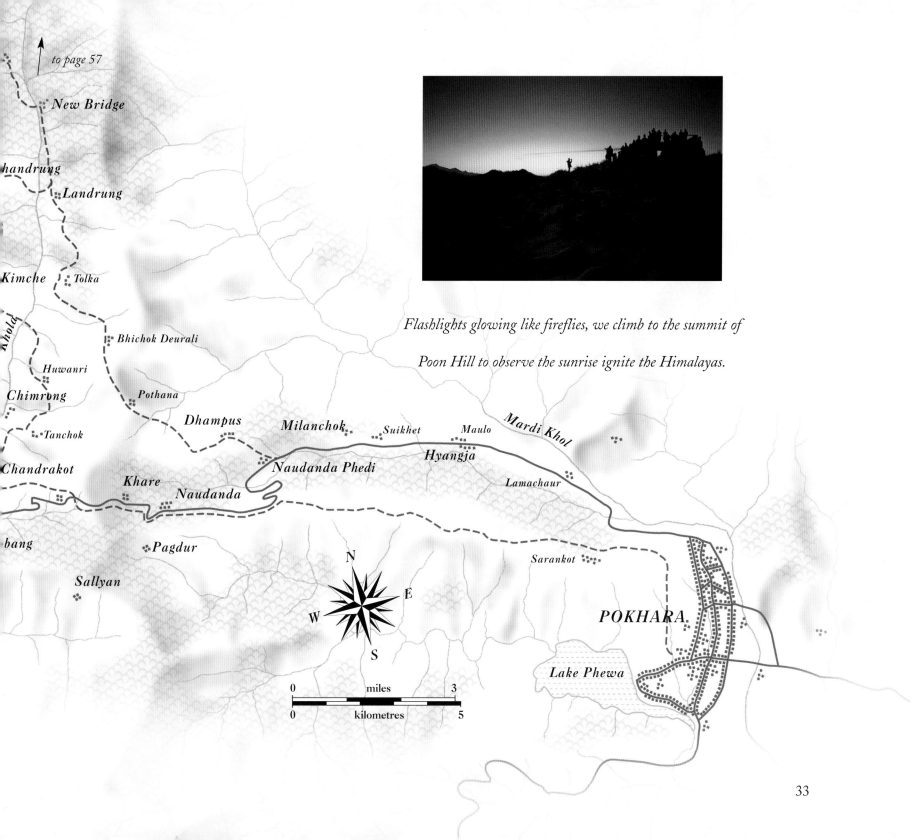

to page 57

New Bridge

handrung

Landrung

Kimche   Tolka

Kholq

Bhichok Deurali

Huwanri

Chimrung   Pothana

Tanchok   Dhampus

Chandrakot   Milanchok   Suikhet   Maulo   Mardi Khol

Khare   Naudanda Phedi   Hyangja

Naudanda   Lamachaur

bang   Pagdur

Sallyan   Sarankot

POKHARA

N

W   E   Lake Phewa

S

0   miles   3

0   kilometres   5

Flashlights glowing like fireflies, we climb to the summit of

Poon Hill to observe the sunrise ignite the Himalayas.

or close to their communities, and I was told that it was a disaster. Cheap Indian goods have flooded their own markets, making it impossible for local artisans or craftsmen to compete. Buses to hospitals in town and trucks to transport produce to markets cost money. And perhaps most importantly the lucrative flow of tourists that used to pass through these villages has all but dried up. Tourists often bypass the quaint historic villages of Chandrakot and Birethanti to continue by road to Beni and from there up the Kali Gandaki, or vice versa. These communities' main source of income, tourism, has been curtailed by the arrival of the road; far from being the magical panacea to their problems, their problems have been exacerbated. Wherever there is a road, deforestation takes place along its verges, and ugly shanty villages of corrugated tin sprout like mushrooms. That, of course, is the perspective of a visiting tourist.

On the positive side, there *is* better access to markets, college education is possible from home, and villagers feel more secure with hospitals in easier reach; and communities further into the mountains receive more tourists because of improved access.

Taking advantage of the Chinese-built road and a bus or taxi ride to Naya Pul, where the road intersects the Modi River, it is possible to reach Ghorepani in two days from Pokhara; witnessing the sunrise from Poon Hill early the next morning, and returning to town late that same day is also feasible, although challenging for the knees. What is as little as a three-day trip seemed an incredibly exotic adventure when I first walked from Pokhara along the ridgeline above Lake Phewa to Naudanda. I remember arriving late and exhausted in Chandrakot that second night, strolling through the slumbering village to its furthest edge, to see Annapurna South looming from the upper reaches of the deep Modi Khola Valley, its snow-covered heights shades of steel blue under a rising full moon. Even now, so many years later, I can visualize that impressive scene in all its detail. The following morning we skipped down to the quaint bazaar at Birethanti, and then staggered up the flagstone steps to Hille where a young Nepalese boy, Dipak, enticed us into Dipak Lodge for the night. I recollect sitting around the fire, in what was basically Dipak's

home, eating with his family, and then later lying in bed gazing through the window at the clear night, the stars, and the flickering lights from candles or cooking fires on the other side of the valley. It all seemed so incredibly romantic.

Arriving worn out in Ghorepani the next day, we nevertheless ascended further up towards Poon Hill, to the uppermost lodge, a ramshackle one-room affair full of smoke. This would allow us the luxury of sleeping in as long as possible. We went to bed early, and well before dawn, stumbling in the dark at the front of a procession of flashlights glowing like fireflies, climbed to the summit of Poon Hill to observe the sunrise ignite the Himalayas. The views of Dauligiri, and the Annapurnas, are illuminated from the top down as the sun rises while to the south (and perhaps even more impressive) are the receding summits of foothills floating above the ground-hugging mist, disappearing into the vastness of pale blue that is the Indian sub-continent.

We descended, spent the night in a wooden shack that then comprised Tadapani, and continued to the idyllic village of Ghandrung before crossing the Modi River to walk back to Pokhara. The trip took us almost ten days and I was hooked on the Himalayan experience; yet this was just a hint of the attachment I would come to feel for these mountains and their people.

I returned to Dipak Lodge in Hille at the end of completing the Circuit recently. Dipak Lodge had expanded, almost unrecognizable from the home I had stayed at, and Dipak, his mother reported sadly, was now a young man seeking his fortune in Hong Kong.

The ramshackle wooden lodge we had stayed in on the way up to the summit of Poon Hill has been demolished and the villagers in Ghorepani have made a communal decision to stop the encroachment of new lodges above Ghorepani itself. Now there is a viewing platform at the summit of Poon Hill, but tourism growth in Ghorepani seems to have slowed with many trekkers opting to take the easier route from Tatopani, following the Kali Gandaki Valley south, to catch the bus at Beni, rather than climbing over the Ghorepani Pass.

Instead of heading straight back down to Birethanti, a small

Peace temple, Pokhara

loop through dense rhododendron forest via Tadapani and Ghandrung provides a relatively easy and genuine insight into rural Nepal. The new stone lodges (one could hardly call these purpose-built buildings teahouses) in Tadapani are attractively constructed, affording spectacular sunset views down the Modi Khola Valley and across to Machhapuchhre, the Fish Tail.

Ghandrung, despite the increasing wealth of its inhabitants, remains one of the most picturesque villages in the Annapurnas, with sun-filled flagstone courtyards and terraced fields below, marred only by one reinforced concrete lodge located at the southern edge of this traditional Gurung settlement. ACAP is sensitizing the people of the Annapurnas to the fact that buildings

of reinforced concrete and corrugated tin roofs, while efficient and cheap to construct, also denigrate the architectural aesthetics of traditional villages.

As a reaction to our sanitized, packaged, automated, high tech, complex world, I have often considered getting back to basics, staying for some weeks in a simple village like Ghandrung, witnessing the cycles of life and the seasons, the daily chores that must be performed, the production of food: harvesting, threshing, winnowing, grinding and storing the grain, fertilizing the fields with compost from the animal stalls, while the sun and clouds perform their daily sleights of hand over Annapurna South, Hiunchuli and Machhapuchhre.

I dream of getting off this whirling financial merry-go-round,

of taking a break somewhere where life is more vivid and intense.

My only plan is to be home, in two-and-a-half months, in time

for Christmas.

Left: Store front, Lakeside, Pokhara

Above: Cleaning up, barber shop, Lakeside, Pokhara

The snow-capped peaks of the Annapurnas reflect the orange morning light, as clear and postcard-perfect as can be.

Mist rises off the mirror-smooth waters of Lake Phewa. Like vapour from dry ice on a theatre stage, the effect is melodramatic.

Left: Lake Phewa reflecting Machhapuchhre
Right: Boatman, Lake Phewa, Pokhara

"Namaste!" "Namaste," I reply, "I salute the god within you."

Her smile is devastating. She has chubby cheeks, a sweet smile,

and eyes that sparkle with humour. "Lemon tea?" she asks.

It occurs to me that never in my life have I been away from

vehicles for such an extended period. It was easier to adjust to the

culture shock of entering the isolation of the mountains than it is

to return to civilization.

Left and below: Pokhara Valley

Over and over again I have discovered, and had to rediscover: the simpler life is the better. The most elementary pleasures give the greatest rewards.

One of the legions of porters who have carried salt, rice and other basic trading goods up and down these valleys for centuries, crossing borders, oblivious to the boundaries relatively recently defined by Western powers.

Left: Bamboo swing put up during the ten-day Dasain festival in October/November

Above: Porter, Naudanda, looking south

The Fish Tail materializes and evaporates behind puffy vapour. From the uppermost lodge, I spend the rest of the afternoon in splendid isolation, admiring the clouds perform artful tricks over mountains.

Machhapuchhre from Dhampus

44

Without question, the road will destroy the natural beauty of the region. The balance of the delicate ecosystem of the Kali Gandaki, and the vulnerable culture of its diverse people, will be radically changed.

I pass her by, feeling sorry for the woman, her head bent down against the load, perspiration dripping off her face. I am doing this out of choice, as a holiday, and for fun. She faces a lifetime of this daily drudgery, yet she can still laugh about it.

Above, left and right: Sarankot

Drums and Nepali folk songs in the distance send me off to a deep sleep, dreaming of Nepal and the Annapurnas.

We walk again through thick forest and occasionally we are afforded views to the south, along valleys crimson with the autumn colours of rhododendron forest.

Left: Musicians and dancers, Sarankot
Above: Rhododendron forest, Ghorepani

The little girl's eyes light up every time she comes through the doors to serve us food.

Left: Young girl, Pokhara Valley
Above: Teahouse, Ghorepani

A young Poon girl, her brother and a pretty girl helper, run the lodge. The atmosphere is friendly and relaxed. Dal bhaat is ready, and we stuff ourselves, replacing calories burnt all day, climbing six hours, non-stop, from the bottom of the Kali Gandaki.

POON HILL

Classic pillars of Jesus Rays reach from

the clouds to light up the valley. I almost

expect Him to appear between the

billowing sunbursts before, once again,

I am drawn back into the mountains to

unshackle the pedestrian bonds of

humanity, and become closer with the

awesome nature surrounding me.

Looking north-east from Poon Hill over Ghorepani,
with Annapurna South on the left and Machhapuchhre
in the distance

I realize the awful implications of being a cripple in this countryside, with no wheels, not even a chance of using a wheelchair with any degree of practicality.

At the summit of Poon Hill there is a growing crowd of trekkers. Where did they all come from? We had seen hardly anyone in the village yesterday evening, and our lodge is empty. There is no "sunrise". At least, there is no ball of fire exploding out of the horizon, but the subtle morning light is beautiful nonetheless.

Left: Polio victim
Right: Poon Hill summit, looking east

ANNAPURNA SANCTUARY

More strenuous than Poon Hill, with a more intimate feeling for these mountains, is the climb into the amphitheatre of the Annapurna Sanctuary. Also achieved relatively quickly by walking straight up the Modi River from Naya Pul/Birethanti to Ghandrung and then Chomrong, and hence to Annapurna Base Camp at 4,130 m/13,550 ft, before descending again, this excursion can be done in as little as a week from Pokhara, although such a limited time does not allow for acclimatization to high altitudes. A more sensible route, taking a little longer, would be to walk up to Poon Hill and cross to Tadapani, before heading through the mysterious rhododendron forest where there are monkey and deer, to Chomrong. It's worth staying more than a day in Chomrong, not only for the food – nak cheese pizza baked in a tin oven – but also for the views.

There is little cultural merit as such to the walk from Chomrong into the Sanctuary. Historically there were no villages here, only cave shelters used by goatherds when they took their flocks into the Sanctuary for summer pasture. Chomrong is the last village before the long climb up the narrow defile that gives entry into the Annapurna Sanctuary. From Chomrong up to Annapurna Base Camp, the facilities and food along a string of lodges become more basic.

On my most recent incursion into the Sanctuary in mid-December, I walked up from Chomrong to Annapurna Base Camp carrying my own heavy backpack, bypassing five recent avalanches that had slid with dramatic effect down the precipitous flanks of Hiunchuli, perched so far above that the mountain itself is concealed beyond its icy ramparts. The avalanches slowed me down, but after five weeks walking around the Circuit, despite my propensity for altitude sickness, the change in elevation of almost

2,000 m/6,560 ft in twelve hours had no affect, although the last hour was spent walking in heavy snow and almost in total darkness. The frozen path was not easy to discern and often I stepped into virgin snow on either side and sank up to my thigh. I had to remove my pack, extricate myself, step on the more solid snow of the trampled path, and hoist my backpack on again. I walked into a lodge at base camp steaming with the effort of the climb, wearing just a thin thermal long-sleeved undershirt under my pack, despite the cold. I can recollect the startled look on the faces of other trekkers, playing cards at a table in the relative warmth of the lodge, as I stumbled in from the darkness.

To say the view from within the Sanctuary is spectacular is to inadequately describe the experience. Deep within the bosom of the Annapurnas, it is even more impressive to be at the epicentre of these mountains after one has just spent some weeks circling them. A photograph may be worth a thousand words, but no photograph can depict a 360-degree panorama of ten snow-covered peaks soaring almost vertically up to 8,000 m/26,000 ft. Immediately above are Annapurna South, the South Face of Annapurna I, first climbed by Chris Bonington's British expedition in 1970, Fang, Tent Peak and Machhapuchhre, aptly named the Fish Tail, perhaps the most beautifully formed peak of all. The fact that the fluted columns leading to this summit have never been scaled lends it an enchanting aspect. Stepping out of the confines of the lodge into the frigid night air and staring up in awe at the surrounding summits bathed in the steel-blue of moonlight, it seems nothing short of a fairytale that this child's vision of a perfect mountain should remain unsullied when all the other peaks, and even the moon floating above, have been "conquered" by man.

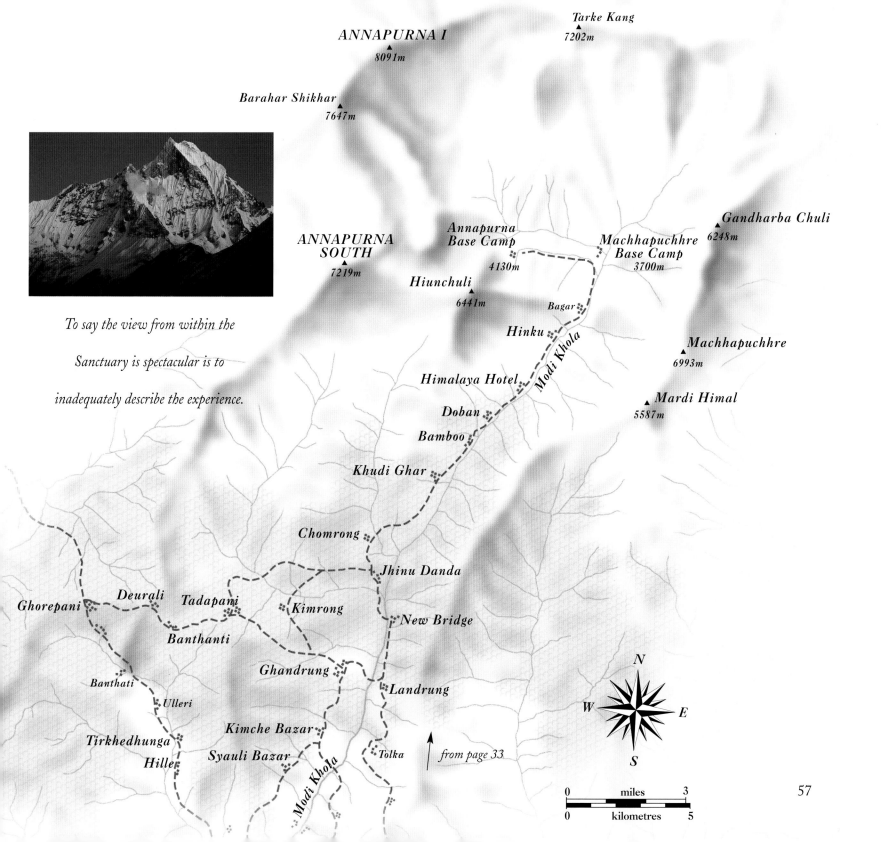

ANNAPURNA I
8091m

Tarke Kang
7202m

Barahar Shikhar
7647m

To say the view from within the

Sanctuary is spectacular is to

inadequately describe the experience.

Gandharba Chuli
6248m

ANNAPURNA
SOUTH
7219m

Annapurna
Base Camp
4130m

Machhapuchhre
Base Camp
3700m

Hiunchuli
6441m

Bagar

Hinku

Machhapuchhre
6993m

Modi Khola

Himalaya Hotel

Mardi Himal
5587m

Doban

Bamboo

Khudi Ghar

Chomrong

Jhinu Danda

Ghorepani

Deurali

Tadapani

Kimrong

New Bridge

Banthanti

Ghandrung

Landrung

Banthati

Ulleri

Kimche Bazar

Tirkhedhunga

Syauli Bazar

Tolka

from page 33

Hille

Modi Khola

N

W   E

S

0   miles   3

0   kilometres   5

Within twenty minutes' walk I could be back on a road, with vehicles, on the fringes of civilization. The narrow sides of the river shelter the village of Birethanti from the visible and audible aspects of the civilized world.

A man whistles to his oxen to thresh the grain on the dusty earth. From two fields below the sound of the men singing as they work wafts on the wind.

Ghandrung is the best-preserved Gurung village in the area. The lodges are on the outskirts, leaving the original village itself intact.

Above and left: Sawing planks of wood, and oxen threshing grain, en route from Birethanti
Right: Sunrise, Ghandrung, looking south-east

I remove sweat-soaked boots and cardboard-stiff socks and let them dry in the sun beside my puckered feet.

Walking under the thick canopy of foliage, I hear a noise and stop to listen. An animal? The forests are full of monkeys and deer. I walk towards the direction of the sound, then hear another noise, behind. I hesitate and listen again for more sounds, but there is nothing.

Annapurna Base Camp is at the centre of a huge amphitheatre of Himalayan mountains comprising Annapurna South, Machhapuchhre, Annapurna I and lesser peaks. For well over a month I have been circling these mountains on the outside. Now I am to become intimately familiar within the bosom of the Sanctuary.

Above: Tadapani
Left: Rhododendron forest en route from Ghorepani to Ghandrung
Right: Walking between Machhapuchhre Base Camp and Annapurna Base Camp, looking east; Machhapuchhre, the Fish Tail, above

As I climb higher into the Sanctuary, out of the narrow defile of the Modi Khola gorge, I am not sure which peak is which, for I have never seen them from this angle before.

Despite the bone-penetrating cold, I cannot stop watching the transformation of these mountains as the clouds disappear from the peaks, and the angled, softer evening light reveals every detail on the mountain walls. The yellow light turns to orange, then pink, then red.

Above: Ascending to Annapurna Base Camp, the south face of Annapurna I in the background, looking north-west

Right: Machhapuchhre seen from Annapurna Base Camp at sunset, looking east

The tide of bright yellow leaks into the craggy dark mountain faces, draining the shadows. Within a short time the mountains radiate white so strongly it hurts the eyes.

Machhapuchhre looms way overhead again as I slip back into the claustrophobic confines of the gorge. Then the intimate views of Annapurnas I and South are gone as I descend and disappear into the wall of mountains.

Left: Annapurna I, South Face, seen from Annapurna Base Camp at dawn, looking north
Above: Modi Khola gorge seen from the Annapurna Sanctuary, looking south

Nothing happened, but so much

happened. What has happened has been

within. I have changed.

Below Birethanti, looking north, with Machhapuchhre
in the distance

THE PILGRIM ROUTE TO MUKTINATH

Pilgrims have embarked on the spectacular walk through the deepest gorge in the world, carved between Dhauligiri and Annapurna I, to the holy pilgrimage site of Muktinath, for thousands of years. This trek is made more accessible both by the road up to Beni and the numerous flights that service the Jomsom airstrip early each day before the vicious Kali Gandaki winds pick up by mid-morning.

The Thakalis have established the tradition of hospitality to passing traders for centuries along the Thak Khola stretch of the Kali Gandaki between Tatopani and Jomsom. The gastronomic delicacies offered at inns in traditional villages such as Tatopani, Tukuche and Marpha are good enough to cater to even the discerning taste of a post-Thorong La Epicurean. This section of the Annapurna Circuit has been referred to disparagingly as the "Apple Pie and Coca Cola Trail", but for those who have walked through Manang over the Thorong Pass, or even over the pass at Ghorepani below Poon Hill, there is nothing offensive about eating freshly made apple pie, or nak cheese pizza.

Tatopani ("tato" means "hot" and "pani" means "water") is one stop everyone looks forward to. Tatopani is a resort-like village where life is comfortable enough to contemplate staying more than a night. In this tropical setting, with luxuriant bananas,

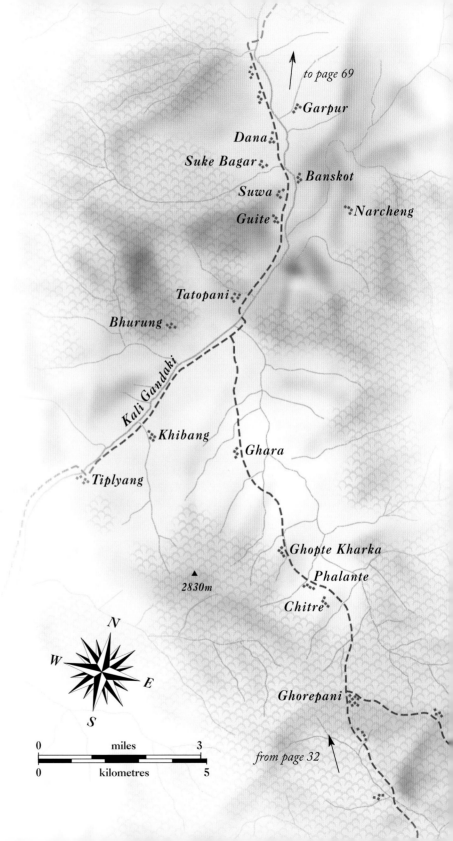

to page 69

Garpur

Dana

Suke Bagar

Banskot

Suwa

Narcheng

Guite

Tatopani

Bhurung

Kali Gandaki

Khibang

Ghara

Tiplyang

2830m

Ghopte Kharka

Phalante

Chitre

N

W

E

S

Ghorepani

from page 32

0   miles   3

0   kilometres   5

Larjung

to page 70

Sauru

Koketani

Dhampugaon

Dhampu

Taglung

Kalopani

Chhoya

Lete

Nimek Danda

Kali Gandaki

▲

Sarpang Dhuri

3904m

N

W

E

S

0   miles   3

0   kilometres   5

Ghasa

Talbagar

Kabre

Bhalebas

Rukse Chhahara

Titre

Garpur

Dana

Suke Bagar

from page 68

guavas, lime, lemon and orange trees in courtyards, and pink-blossomed cherry trees, Tatopani is so enticing it may be difficult to get motivated enough to leave. The restaurants are an occasion to store a few excess calories to compensate for the upcoming, or past, weeks of daily deficiencies. Apart from the fabled cakes and good food, there are two hot spring pools, and an opportunity to soak away blisters, grime, and sore muscles. There's nothing quite as satisfying as basking in the scalding water with a cold beer in hand, staring up the valley at Nilgiri's peaks lit by the setting sun. Whether heading upstream, or back to Pokhara via Ghorepani, the impending climbs are intimidating enough to reconsider an extra soak in the hot pools, a procrastinating browse through the used book stores, followed by lunch and a siesta, then dinner and another good night's sleep before climbing the steep ascent north into the Himalayas or south to Ghorepani.

Heading north, slipping through the deepest canyon in the world, the vegetation changes dramatically within a short distance. Out of the awesome abyss and into the rain shadow north of the Himalayas, the landscape shifts to arid browns. There are no longer any buffalo, and the profusion of birds and insects – butterflies, grasshoppers and dragonflies – quietly disappear. The guidebooks tell you that not only is this a pivotal divide between the Alpine and sub-Alpine zones to the north, and the sub-tropical and tropical zones to the south, but also a bio-geographical divide between east and west, the extreme range of the Palaearctic and Oriental distribution of animals, plants and birdlife.

The steep-sided gorges tightly embracing a torrent of river water suddenly open to a wide riverbed braided by sparkling streams snaking from side to side, slithering over shining cobbles. Scattered along the riverbed are shaligrams, smooth round black stones, like prehistoric rock eggs which, when successfully broken open, reveal fossilized ammonites, sea creatures that lived on the seabed over 100 million years ago. Hindus revere these stones as representative of the god Vishnu; hence the shaligrams, and the river too, are sacred.

Further upstream is Tukuche, the ancient trading centre where mule trains from the south, carrying grains and other goods, met

69

yak caravans from the north, carrying rock salt and turquoise. The substantial warehouses have for the most part deteriorated as the trade into Tibet all but stopped, but tourism has injected new life into these magnificent buildings built around central courtyards.

Before reaching the staging point of bustling Jomsom is the whitewashed and flagstone-lined village of Marpha, celebrated for offerings of apple pies and other gastronomic delights. Signs on the Thakali bhattis proclaim: "Hot shower – Best Fooding and Lodging in cheap rate. Italian, Mexican, Continental Food".

I am struck by the equanimity with which trekkers order their dinners, fully expecting recognizable meals to arrive out of these medieval, teenage-run kitchens. Despite the apparent chaos in the scullery, pizza, fried rice, spring rolls, burritos and lasagne are served in identifiable form.

Persistent gusts pelt dust and grit, kicked up by the hooves of caravans of somnambulant mules, colourful yak-tail head tresses blown horizontal as they meander timelessly through Jomsom's main drag, ringing brass neck bells intermingling with the roar of the wind.

Above lammergeyers soar easily on thermals, static wings spanning 3 m/10 ft. Alpine choughs cavort wildly in the wind, elevated by unseen currents of air only to fold back their wings, plummeting back to earth where they happily congregate in a field before wheeling up into the heavens to repeat the whole process.

Red House Lodge, an old Khampa hideout with its own two-storey gold Buddha in the heart of Kagbeni, is a typically archaic affair run with alarming eccentricity and efficiency by two giggling sisters and an assortment of children. By comparison, Nilgiri Lodge, despite the mummified yak's head over the doorway, has private rooms with carpets and attached Western-style flush toilets, showers and an immaculate kitchen. The red gompa and ruined fort in the centre of this walled community are testaments to the strategic location this fortified village maintained at the confluence of the Dzong River and the Kali Gandaki. The primitive male and female mud effigies guarding the gates here and at Jharkot are enduring reminders of the animist leanings of these people, while the electrical poles that seem to increasingly

from page 69

Marpha

Tukuche

Kali Gandaki

Sauru

Larjung

Koketani

Taglung

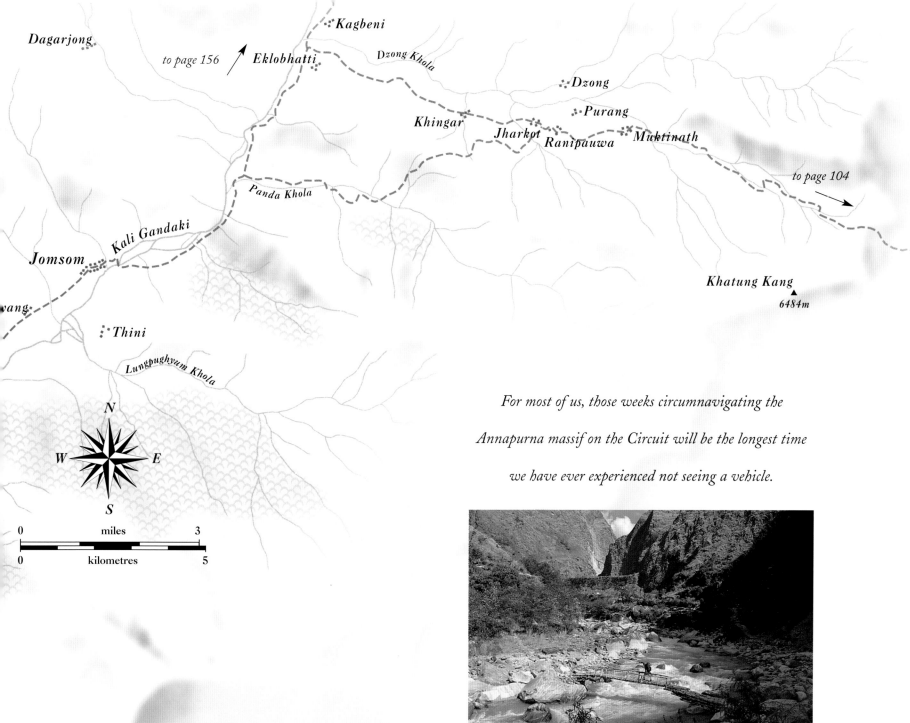

Dagarjong

to page 156

Kagbeni

Eklobhatti

Dzong Khola

Dzong

Khingar

Purang

Jharkot

Muktinath

Ranipauwa

Panda Khola

to page 104

Jomsom

Kali Gandaki

Khatung Kang
6484m

vang

Thini

Lungpughyum Khola

N

W   E

S

0   miles   3

0   kilometres   5

For most of us, those weeks circumnavigating the
Annapurna massif on the Circuit will be the longest time
we have ever experienced not seeing a vehicle.

dominate the choicest of vistas are a reminder of how, even here, the contemporary world is making its inevitable intrusion.

For most of us, those weeks circumnavigating the Annapurna massif will be the longest time we have ever experienced not seeing a vehicle or, for that matter, a wheel. No engines, no exhaust, no blaring horns. Only the high-pitched cries and whistles of men encouraging their dzo to plough the earth, the clicking hooves of mules and donkeys sharing the path, the blowing huff of a tired pony, the trickling water of a stream or the roar of the river below, the sharp crack followed by a rolling grumble, like thunder, as an overhanging glacier falls from its precarious perch. But this too is changing as the two trailheads extend north towards the Himalayas. In the medieval labyrinth of narrow alleys and courtyards of the crumbling mud homes that comprise Kagbeni, I was astounded to come across children who had never seen anything with wheels in their lives before, not even a bullock cart, nonchalantly taking it in turns to cycle a child's mountain bike through their village. That same day I witnessed on the Kali Gandaki, bouncing over the round stones of the riverbed, two groaning tractors that had been helicoptered in to Jomsom, beeping their horns, noisily ferrying supplies to Chele in Upper Mustang.

Stretching east from Kagbeni along the Dzong Valley are three easily recognizable medieval fortress villages reminiscent in many ways of medieval Europe. "Dzong" means "fort" in Tibetan and the Dzong Valley is as far north into Mustang Westerners may go now without paying the high fees entailed trekking further in to Lomanthang, and Upper Mustang. These ancient fortresses made of rammed mud and straw are abandoned sentinels of a bygone era.

The Dzong Valley between Kagbeni and Jharkot, and the "high route" between Upper Pisang and Braga, are my favourite stretches of the Annapurna Circuit. With their spectacular open views, desert-like terrain, hardy people, and fortress homes and villages, there is a haunting beauty about these places. I can never seem to get enough of this spectacular valley affording vistas into Upper Mustang, the Himalayas, and fortress villages on either side

of a valley laced with thousands of caves formed as much as 2,000 years ago by Neolithic troglodytes who inhabited these apartment-like dwellings. Below the grotto-like abodes are the skeletal outlines of buildings and terraced fields, now decaying relics in an empty gorge, remnants of a time when water was plentiful and the terraced fields fertile.

The temples of Muktinath are contained within a walled oasis of springs and poplars. Here 108 brass waterspouts shaped in the form of animals' heads spew holy waters into the courtyard around the Vishnu Temple where scantily clad sadhus, who have made the pilgrimage from India, rest beside the pools or within the temple grounds. The nearby Jwala Mai Temple is built around a cavity where flames burn out of the stone, earth and spring, making this site, after Pashupatinath, one of the holiest of sites for Hindus.

It is not difficult to imagine the awe of early wanderers after weeks of climbing the Kali Gandaki, arriving at this holy site situated at the foot of the Khatung Kang, looming some 2,000 m/6,000 ft overhead. The setting does exude a sense of being the home of the gods. In this day of satellite television, DVDs, personal computers, CD-ROMs and nuclear bombs, the flickering blue flames of Muktinath are not particularly impressive, but they must have seemed incredibly auspicious to people 2,000 years ago. These flames ignite my imagination for what this place must have been to the countless pilgrims who have come here, but for me there is no religious fervour.

Listening to the sounds of the stream, smelling the earthy freshness of the air, I open my eyes and absorb the crisp light, feel the rough texture of the wood I sit on, taste the cold water, sense the gentle breeze on my sun-warmed body. This is a spiritual experience for me and it has nothing to do with the flickering flames or the four-armed statue waving angrily within the pagoda temple. Sitting in the warm speckled sunlight under the banyan, peepul and poplar trees, beside the babbling spring-fed stream, I feel a sense of freedom, peacefulness, of harmony within and without, as if my spirit and body are catching up with each other.

There are two natural hot spring-fed pools at Tatopani. Half a dozen partially submerged trekkers' faces float amid the swirling stream. As the day progresses, dozens of trekkers arrive and immerse themselves in the pools. The water gets murkier but we are addicted to the fix of a shower or hot bath, and clean bodies.

A colourfully dressed wedding party, accompanied by a local drum band, plays Nepalese folk music.

Above: Hot springs at Tatopani, looking south
Right: Wedding at a small hamlet above Tatopani

Tramping around the Himalayas with a heavy backpack, I have been as happy as I could ever be. I have enjoyed life with an intensity I have not experienced in the last couple of years. I lived for the moment. I have learned much from the materially poor but spiritually affluent people living very simply in the Annapurnas.

The sun reflects off the flagstone path which winds its way through the colourful plots and becomes lost in the slate-stone rooftops of village houses.

Left: Between Lete and Kalopani, looking south
Above: Between Koketani and Larjung, looking south

A blast of wind down the valley stirs my expectations and drives me forward; but strangely there is no immediate objective, just a vague sense of going higher, into the Himalayas.

A caravan of dzopkio knock me about as they pass. They seem to do this purposely, and I have learnt to stay on the inside of the track.

Left: Crossing the Kali Gandaki at Larjung, looking north-west
Above: En route from Khobang to Tukuche

Tukuche was the principal trading post on the Kali Gandaki for hundreds of years, where bhotia from the north brought down Tibetan rock salt carried by yak and sheep and returned with rice and grains and goods.

Above: Street scene, Tukuche
Opposite: Gompa at Tukuche, looking south

The sun's rays penetrate through the gaps in the mountains, hitting the valley on the opposite side, where the inevitable chorten or small gompa would seem to have been built specifically to benefit from their position: the hot sun warms the ground, and the white coating of frost melts quickly.

I am descending through the deepest canyon of the world,

bounded on either side by the Himalayas. Winter recedes

confusingly almost before we have got used to its arrival,

and summer scenes once again charge the senses.

Poverty is not fun.

Left: Looking south to Tukuche
Above: Collecting dung outside Marpha

A yakherd drives several yak along a narrow ridge where they are momentarily silhouetted against the mountains, imprinted indelibly like a black-and-white photograph on my mind.

A chorten on the outskirts of Marpha signals the whitewashed village and the main, intricately patterned, flagstone-lined passageway.

I watch them for a long time as they walk down the rock-strewn bed of the Kali Gandaki. A rider on a horse passes them heading in my direction, and then they are gone, for ever, disappearing into the vastness of the mountains.

Opposite: Dzopkio outside Marpha, looking south
Above: Street scene, Marpha
Left: En route from Jomsom to Kagbeni, looking south

*At the bottom of the Dzong Khola, the
Fortress River, lies the village of
Kagbeni on the eastern bank of the Kali
Gandaki.*

*Run by two Tibetan women who cannot
stop laughing at the slightest excuse, Red
House Lodge has a peculiar charm. The
rooms are a jumble of mismatched
cubicles. On the roof a glass-enclosed
"conservatory" is filled with trekkers
reading in the fading daylight.*

*The great canyon of the Kali Gandaki
has been one of the major passageways
linking the high Tibetan plateau with the
lowlands of India for centuries, perhaps
even thousands of years.*

Left: Looking north towards Eklobhatti and Kagbeni
Top: Looking south from Kagbeni to Nilgiri
Above: Red House Lodge, Kagbeni

85

From the vantage point of Kagbeni, it must appear as if the sun streams straight out of Muktinath. The autumn leaves of the trees in the oases of the valley below absorb the intense morning light, colourful against the brown of the surrounding rocks.

The architecture differs from anything we have seen so far. Stone buildings, low and fat, with larger riven wood shingles on horizontal roofs, held down by boulders. Yak skulls adorn the entranceways.

Above: Looking east towards Thorong La from Kagbeni
Left: Lodge exterior, Kagbeni

Nepal still has one of the highest death rates among children under five years of any country in the world. By many standards of measurement, it is one of the poorest countries in the world; a fact conveniently forgotten when we become seduced by friendly and apparently happy inhabitants of idyllic Rousseau-like villages.

Right: Girl in Kagbeni

For societies so dependent on modern methods of transport, 60 miles across the roadless Himals seems unimaginable today. Five hundred years ago the distance between Jumla and Mustang would have meant nothing.

Kagbeni's buildings, secured within a protective perimeter of walls, are clumped around its red ochre-washed gompa and dzong fortress.

Above: Man from Jumla

Right: Looking west towards the walled fortress village of Kagbeni at the confluence of the Dzong River and the Kali Gandaki, Upper Mustang to the north

One key aspect of tourism in these mountains is the lack of vehicles. No matter how rich the tourists, we all have to use our own two feet to walk in this mountainous environment, just as the locals do. It is the great equalizer.

Right: Looking east towards Jharkot, Muktinath and Thorong La

90

A decrepit, dusty man peers through prescription glasses as thick as the bottoms of Coca-Cola bottles.

Above: Jharkot, looking north-east
Left: Old man carding and spinning raw wool in pilgrimage hostel, Ranipauwa

Surrounding Jharkot, brown fields lie fallow now the harvest of buckwheat, barley and maize has been reaped. Within weeks I have almost witnessed a complete season, from the verdant green paddy growing around Dumre, to the dry fallow fields being prepared for next year's crop before the arrival of winter. Summer and winter collided.

Eroded yellow cliffs on the other side of the Dzong Valley are riddled with holes like Swiss cheese. I surmise they must be man-made caves, thousands of them. Who lived in here? Did monks come to pray around this holiest of sites? Do the caves demarcate the limits of two ancient kingdoms, providing protection in the case of hostilities?

A Tibetan mandala painting on the wall of the Jharkot gompa depicts the essential aspects of the Buddha's teachings. It includes a pig, a cock and a snake, respectively representing the three cardinal faults of delusion, passion and hatred.

Left: Dzong Valley near Jharkot, looking north
Above: Temple exterior, Jharkot

The Dzong Valley lies far below, beautiful in the evening sun.

The sun catches the colours on the trees and the ochre gompas of the villages of Jharkot and Dzong.

Above: Dzong, seen from Jharkot, looking north

Right: Jharkot, looking west, seen from the route to Muktinath

Muktinath has been a pilgrimage site for at least 2,000 years because of holy flames that burn out of the ground, rocks and spring. Behind the temple 108 elephant and cow heads spew effervescent water, giving the Tibetan name for Muktinath, Chu Mig Gya Tsa Gye, meaning "the 108 springs".

The dilapidated condition of the Jwala Mai Temple in which the miraculous flames burn is rather a surprise in the context of the religious significance of Muktinath.

Left: Vishnu Temple, Muktinath
Above: Jwala Mai Temple, Muktinath

BESISAHAR TO THORONG LA

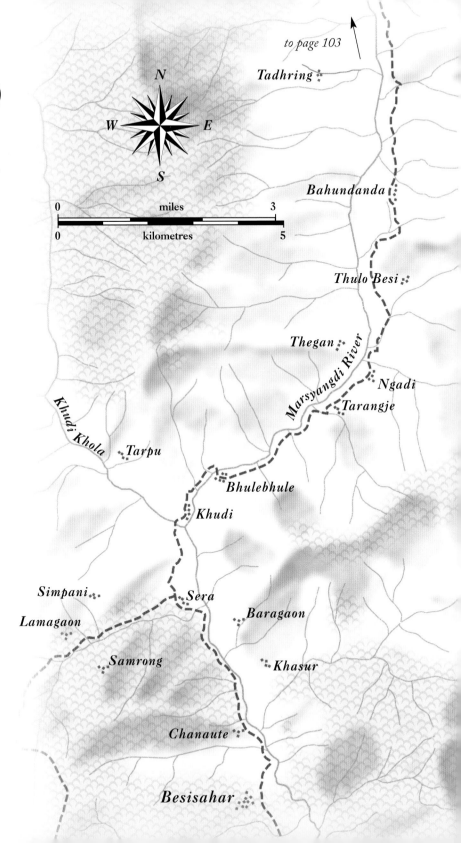

to page 103

Without a doubt, the Annapurna Circuit is the classic hiking route. Nowhere else can one encounter such a variation in climate, geography, flora or fauna, where a confusing mixture of ethnic groups live out a lifestyle largely unchanged for centuries. Nepal was a sequestered kingdom completely cut off from the outside world until the 1950s. Manang and the upper reaches of Mustang were restricted areas until the 1970s when the CIA stopped backing the Tibetan Khampa refugees' incursions into Chinese-occupied Tibet from their bases here. Once these two districts were no longer off-limits, it was only a matter of time before the trekking expeditions offered the Annapurna Circuit, combining the ancient trails up the Marsyangdi River with the historic route along the Kali Gandaki, separated by the 5,416-m/17,769-ft Thorong Pass.

Most of the almost 10,000 trekkers who tackle the Annapurna Circuit annually do so counter-clockwise because of the lack of availability of accommodation from Muktinath in Mustang to the Thorong Pass 1,600 m/5,300 ft above. On the Manang side, trekking from east to west or counter-clockwise, there is accommodation at Thorong Phedi, a less daunting 966 m/3,170 ft below the pass. More recently built accommodation at Upper Thorong Phedi can reduce that final day's climb over the pass by another 300 m/1,000 ft.

The bhattis or teahouses on this side of the Thorong La are more basic affairs where common dormitories and platform beds were, until recently, the norm. Toilets were often not provided and food was basically dal bhaat, rice and lentils, the only meal on offer. Teahouses were smoke-filled rickety structures that provided a roof over one's head and not much else.

Climbing up the Marsyangdi River into the deep gorges between the Himalayas, a Buddhist world inhabited primarily by Mongolian types gradually replaces the largely Hindu/Caucasian ethnic groups of the lower elevations. From the lush paddy fields and tropical heat and humidity of the foothills, to the colder, arid, wintery environment on the north side of the Annapurnas, the transition over a period of a week's hiking is complete. Gone are the thick jungle-like bamboo and rhododendron forests and the landscaped terraces of the rice fields. The earth becomes parched brown, dominated on the craggy mountain slopes by chir pines. Even the architecture of the homes changes as the last of the water buffalo are seen, and the first of the dzopkio, a cross between a cow and a yak, and then finally at the upper reaches of the Manang Valley the enormous full-blooded Tibetan yak.

Beyond the District headquarters of Chame is the village of Bhratang, simply a cluster of a few buildings preceded by a long mani wall containing stone tablets with Tibetan inscriptions and a chorten built over the path. Before the Annapurna Circuit was opened up to foreign trekkers, "Khampa" refugees inhabited Bhratang.

Long known as unruly rebels and bandits from the Kham province of Tibet, the Khampas were to become Tibet's last hope for freedom, as the tall and powerfully built warriors waged a rearguard action for many years against the occupying forces of the Chinese Communists. Eventually forced to retreat to bases in Manang and Mustang, internationally recognized as lying within the borders of Nepal, they were protected against retaliation from the Chinese invaders. From these bases, with American support, they continued to strike at the Chinese army, but this covert assistance was not so much for Tibet's freedom as it was part of American strategy to destabilize Communist governments all over the world.

The "high route" between Upper Pisang and Braga/Manang is the highlight of the Circuit for me and yet, setting out in late November or early December, I rarely encounter other trekkers

here. Diverting only an extra 500 m/1,600 ft above the main trail on the valley bottom, the "high route" provides not only more spectacular views of the Annapurnas, but also offers an authentic cultural experience through staying in the fortress-like homes of typical medieval "Tibetan" villages. These bunker-like homes, accessed by a notched tree trunk worn smooth by the passage of hands and feet, are three storeys high. The ground floor is an enclosed courtyard for animals; the second floor is living quarters and kitchen. The upper level, also accessed by a tree trunk, is used to winnow and store grain. During daylight, the upper level serves as the general work area, the fuel-wood stored on the perimeter of the roof serving as a protective wall to form a suntrap.

A more ambitious excursion, climbing even higher, above Upper Pisang towards Pisang Peak, provides a stunning perspective up and down the valley. I stay at least a night in each of Upper Pisang, Ghyaru and Ngwal on the "high route", and then, before heading down towards Braga, contour up, passing several impressive chortens and manis (a wall full of stones carved with the Tibetan Buddhist prayer) and a new Buddhist monastery. All these extra nights spent at higher altitudes contribute to the acclimatization process.

One often passes old women or men swinging their prayer wheels of silver, brass, coral, turquoise and wood. The block-printed prayers contained within the cylinder body are offered to the deities invoked. The momentum of a metal ball on the end of a short chain keeps the wheel spinning consistently. As if their personal pleas weren't enough, hundreds of prayer flags reach up from poles on rooftops, fluttering their printed entreaties in the breeze. Semi-terraced, apparently barren stony fields descend down the slopes into the valley. The mercurial river snakes far below, its roar now only a dull rumble. Alpine choughs drop out of the heavens, wings folded as if in prayer as they plunge downwards.

Once in Braga or nearby Manang, the last villages before the Thorong Pass, take the occasion to further acclimatize to the high altitude, and make the two-hour hike up to the lama living in a hermitage above Manang who, for a donation, will perform a puja (a

prayer or religious offering), blessing you and tying a red ribbon around your neck, a guaranteed insurance policy for getting over the pass. A stroll across the river to the summer yak pastures near the glacier hanging below Gangapurna is a worthwhile side trip providing an impressive perspective of Manang on the other side of the turquoise glacier-fed lake below. More ambitiously, the Khangsar Valley east, towards Tilicho Lake, offers brilliant vistas and a longer walk; a lodge at the far end of the Khangsar Valley makes viewing Tilicho Lake a possibility. Or take a pony up from Braga to Ice Lake, about the same height as Thorong Phedi. These excursions, apart from being highlights of the Annapurna Circuit, provide ideal opportunities to "climb high and sleep low" in preparation for the climb over the Thorong Pass. Despite my propensity to get acute mountain sickness, by taking this extra time to acclimatize not only do I substantially reduce the risk of suffering cerebral or pulmonary oedema, but I will actually enjoy the walk over the Thorong Pass. Whether my knees endure the interminable descent to Muktinath on the other side is another question.

Tourism in Nepal is big business, and with so few alternative local investment opportunities many individuals and communities are waking up to the fact that building a tourist lodge is, in the long term, one of the safest and most lucrative business ventures open to the Nepalese. The people of Manang have for centuries had special tax concessions giving them the right to import duty free into Nepal, breeding enterprising well-travelled businessmen. These import concessions have been largely withdrawn and many young Manangi are returning to their birthplace with their families to build and run lodges, thus revitalizing their communities. They are giving up the urban rat race in Kathmandu to rekindle the traditions of a dying culture they now recognize as an asset, as well as benefiting from the fresh air and a simpler life.

For example Karma, who left Braga as an infant, owned a restaurant in Kathmandu. He has returned to Braga and talks in terms most Westerners can easily relate to, rediscovering his roots and a healthier environment where the quality of his life in the "countryside" is less stressful than it was in the city. He is the proud owner of a pony and takes an active part in the traditions of

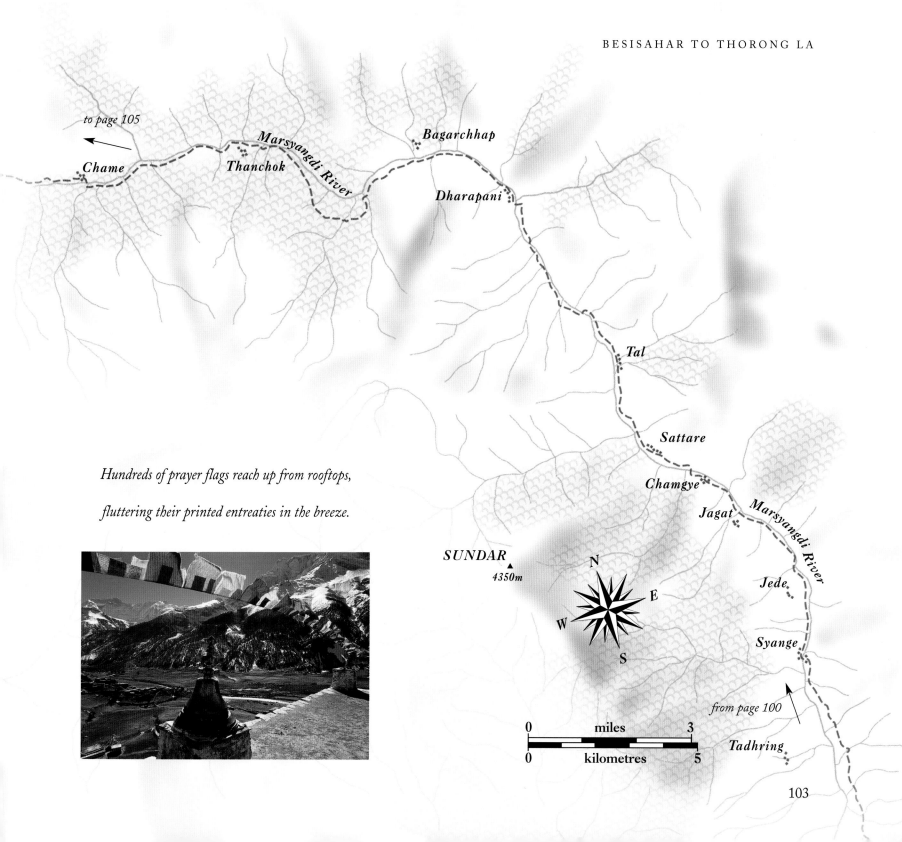

to page 105

Chame

Thanchok

Marsyangdi River

Bagarchhap

Dharapani

Tal

Sattare

Chamgye

Jagat

Marsyangdi River

Jede

Syange

from page 100

Tadhring

Hundreds of prayer flags reach up from rooftops,

fluttering their printed entreaties in the breeze.

SUNDAR
▲
4350m

N
E
W
S

0   miles   3

0   kilometres   5

Manang. His bakery and lodge, and the lodge adjacent to his, are a far cry from the basic facilities available some years ago. Business is good, despite the competition, and the trekking season even in Manang has extended from the October–November period to include most of the winter.

Walking the Manang side of the Annapurna Circuit was an arduous leg with only basic food and lodging available. Lodges have increased in number, and so has the competition, and the quality of service is better, and perhaps nowhere is this more obvious than in Braga, a medieval village clinging to a hillside below a 500-year-old gompa. Braga has lodges not only offering excellent food and accommodation, but also newly baked bread, cinnamon rolls and freshly ground coffee. In nearby Manang there is a huge satellite dish and communications centre with the possibility of phoning home. These developments are mind boggling given the context of the area and the time warp such services and infrastructure represent by comparison to every other aspect of the harsh life here. Walking through Braga or Manang was to take a time machine back 500 years. It still is, except now you can phone home to tell everyone about it and then have a warm Danish pastry over a cup of real coffee.

But the newer lodges also make it difficult for the existing ones. One bhatti I always stay at offers excellent food and services, but has almost no overnight visitors because two or three new lodges in the same village have been written up in the guidebooks, and this one has been overlooked. Similarly, but on a grander scale, in the case of Upper Pisang on the "high route", at least one important guidebook suggested bypassing Upper Pisang and heading straight up to Ghyaru. In Upper Pisang the traditional fortress-homes accessed by log ladders that had been tidied up and converted to take in guests are no longer occupied, and yet for those willing to use their initiative, the homes in Upper Pisang are open.

For the independent trekker, the Annapurna Circuit has

to page 71

become a lot more comfortable, one is less likely to get sick, and it's certainly possible to enjoy the freedom of doing it alone. Organized trekking groups have largely become redundant because it is more comfortable to sleep on a bed in a teahouse than on the ground in a cold tent. The standards of "fooding and lodging" have reached a stage where individual bedrooms are not only typical, but some teahouses even have attached bathrooms. Food is much safer to eat, more varied, and tastier, and sanitation facilities have improved tremendously: most teahouses provide some kind of toilet, no matter how basic.

Despite these "mod cons", it's an achievement to circumnavigate these mountains. Silently struggling under a backpack for weeks is a form of meditation, a chance to catch up to yourself, rediscovering an inner peace, perhaps even a more intimate awareness of who you are. In these mountains, life slows down, allowing the luxury of time and harmony of mind to nurture that essence of being, the nether land between understanding and unconsciousness, the soul.

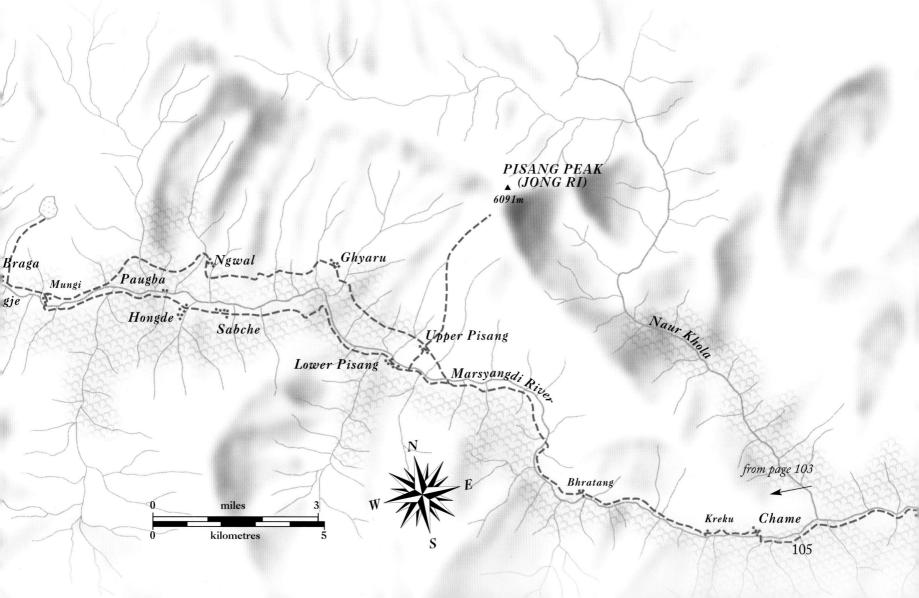

from page 103

For the next couple of months, my worldly possessions are stuffed on my back, as if I were a turtle waddling under its protective carapace. Apart from the vague notion of walking around the Himalayas, I have no targets, no schedule, nowhere to be.

Western pop music blares out of speakers below. The Westerners chatting on the patio, the electric lights, the Western music, it all seems so out of place.

Harnessed waters trickle tamely through glittering channels and irridescent green paddy.

Above: Dumre to Besisahar by bus, looking north
Left: Besisahar looking south
Right: Paddy fields between Besisahar and Bhulebhule

I cross a small bridge over a river full of rocks. Stopping to rest in the middle of the bridge, I listen to the sounds of the rushing water. A brown dipper flits to a rock, its tail flicking up and down, then dives into the fast-flowing current and disappears beneath shards of sunlight reflecting off the rippling waters.

Fees collected from hikers fund the Annapurna Conservation Area Project to the extent that it is self-financing.

The landscape changes. Scarcer villages, fewer rice paddy fields. Terraces are planted with maize and barley.

Left: Khudi, looking north, between Besisahar and Bhulebhule
Top: ACAP checkpoint at Bhulebhule
Right: En route from Ngadi to Bahundanda

A mule train passes through the village. Instead of diesel fumes, the bittersweet smell of the mules' dung, warm and wet, is an insignificant hazard. I step in the middle of a tennis-ball-sized lump of dung, to demonstrate to myself how innocuous it is. Not only harmless and biodegradable, it is also an asset to flora along the route.

I register at the police checkpoint at the bottom of the village, then for the fun of it gallop up the long bob-sleigh run of stone steps in a final manic burst of energy.

Above: Looking south to Usta, between Ngadi and Bahundanda
Right: Police checkpoint just below Bahundanda

110

The rutted trail winds its way into horizontal terraces carved out of the mountainsides, delineating heights as precisely as the contours of a map. Rice fields pour down slopes like molten green lava.

Left: Looking south from Bahundanda
Below: View south on the way up to Bahundanda

113

We reach Syange, a splatter of whitewashed buildings flung against a cliff like vulture droppings.

The tops of the mountains loom high on either side of the hand-carved pathways and staircases creeping along this historic route, which traders from Manang and Tibet have followed for centuries, efficiently expediting cargoes through apparently impenetrable mountains.

Left: Syange, looking north
Right: Bridge at Syange

Dominating his tiny, fragile-looking ankles and knobbly knees, his calf muscles swell like inflated balloons, pulsating veins criss-crossing the calves with each step ascended. Not much more than five foot tall, almost bent double with the weight of his burden, he leans on a thick bamboo pole with each step.

The valley becomes tighter, a narrow gorge with little direct sunlight. A screen of mist lends a perpetual dream-like ambience to the trek.

Above: En route from Jagat to Chamgye, looking south
Right: Buddhist lama, en route from Karte to Tal, looking north

116

I see the mountains framed through the window, tinged by the sunrise for the first time. They seem so close and rise so steeply they block from sight the loftier, snow-covered Himals.

It is cosy in the bhatti, protected from the rain, served hot food and drink. We watch a man producing sausages from the blood, gristle and intestines of a yak.

As we prepare to leave, the bhatti girl hovers around our rooms like a magpie, waiting for us to depart, so she can check the floors and beds for pens, sweeties, rupees and priceless diaries.

Left: Chame, looking north-east
Above: Bhatti at Dharapani
Right: Young girl with younger sibling on her back,
Lower Pisang

A solid sheet of massive rock rises 3,000 ft or more. The smooth escarpment is so steep that its slopes are devoid of vegetation. It is difficult to comprehend the scale of this rock or the earth's forces that have formed it.

I climb higher to a larger building, the village gompa, a Tibetan Buddhist monastery. The rooftop is festooned with vertically aligned Buddhist prayer flags flapping gently in the breeze.

Left: Wall of Paungda Danda, en route from Bhratang to Pisang, looking north-east
Right: Upper Pisang, looking south to the Annapurnas

There is a spirituality about this valley.
Perhaps it is the elevation, the clear blue
sky, the silence, the comfortable warmth of
the sun on the skin in the crisp air.
Perhaps it is because we are so high up we
are just that much closer to the gods.

I stumble half asleep into a typical
Tibetan interior, an open hearth and fire
blazing in the middle of the room, scruffy
children sitting hunched in front of the
flames, hands outstretched.

The village gompa is decorated with
ornately carved wooden window-frames
painted bright colours.

Left: En route from Pisang to Ghyaru, looking west
Above: Teahouse at Ghyaru
Right: Inside the gompa, Ghyaru

I walk through a Buddhist commemorative monument straddling the path, a kani, and spin the cylindrical drums of prayer wheels on the inner walls in a clockwise direction as I pass by.

At a high point in the path, I see the ruins of an ancient fort 600 ft below, straddling a strategic spur on a ridge, dominating the valley.

Left: Exit gate from Ghyaru
Right: Annapurna III, seen between Ghyaru and Ngwal, looking south-west

She is desperately excited and nervous, and

I wonder if she has ever had guests before.

Left: Teahouse, Ngwal
Below: Ngwal, looking east

Although we are about a mile

away from the village, the

whipping of the prayer flags is still

faintly audible in the pervasive

silence of these lofty mountains.

The bhatti owner's daughter asks me "Pen?" "No pen," I reply.

"Sweetie?" she persists. A boy joins us. "Where are you?" He has the

right idea, but forgets to add, "coming from". Stage fright, I suppose.

Above: Children beside a mani wall, Ngwal
Right: Gompa, Ngwal, looking north-west

Alpine choughs drop out of the heavens, wings folded as if in

prayer. Competing yellow-beaked choughs, looking like crows but

smaller, ride the crests of air waves, as if tossed about on invisible

roller-coasters. They too, are spirits floating, diving, twisting,

soaring in the wind.

The last glimmer of the sun glints off the smooth surface of the prayer stones of another mani wall, casting into dark relief their carved inscriptions.

Above: Mani wall outside Ngwal with
Annapurna II behind, looking south-east
Right: Annapurna III at sunrise, from Ngwal,
looking south

The blue-tinged Himals appear so close, every crevice, wrinkle, overhang and column punches out clearly against the dark royal-blue of the pre-dawn sky. The soft light strangely and misleadingly makes it look as if it is possible to take a casual stroll up to the top of these mountains.

Here, only some miles away from the Tibetan border, is a more authentic living "Tibetan" environment than in Tibet itself.

There is almost a physical tugging at my heart leaving this place. One's spirit would be richer if one could be born here, live all one's life here, and die here.

Above: New gompa between Ngwal and Braga, looking south
Right: Braga and Annapurna II, looking south-east from a gompa roof

Front centre is dominated by a golden

Buddha draped in yellow robes with

white kata scarves in his hands.

Left: Inside the gompa, Braga
Above: En route from Braga to the Ice Lake, looking
south-west towards Manang

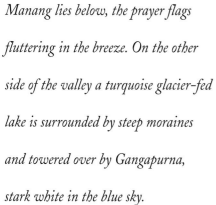

Manang lies below, the prayer flags fluttering in the breeze. On the other side of the valley a turquoise glacier-fed lake is surrounded by steep moraines and towered over by Gangapurna, stark white in the blue sky.

We sit around the dining table. The family live in this one room, centred around a fire in the middle of the floor. Against the far wall are beds, covered in Tibetan carpets, doubling as sofas. Another wall is dominated by a cabinet hewn from heavy planks, riven and smoothed with a hard adze.

Above: Celebrating the birth of a child, Braga bakery

135

The immensity of the mountains is humbling. There are no man-made machines or structures to give a sense of self-importance. We are merely ants, crawling on the surface and wrinkles and folds of the earth, itself only a tiny fragment of the universe.

Light. It is everywhere, reflecting off the mica in the rocks, the leaves, the river, the snow. It seems to enter my soul, brightening the darkest corners of my heart and mind. I have an overwhelming sense of peace.

Left: Annapurna III between Braga and Ice Lake, looking south
Above: Annapurna III from Ice Lake, looking south

137

At the Himalayan Rescue Association's building, the only cement and stone structure in Manang, a daily information session on mountain sickness is given by doctors to trekkers about to cross the Thorong La.

A lama reads and chants from rectangular prayer sheets, occasionally ringing a bell. His features are oriental, almost Chinese.

The gompa is open to view, but the 500-year-old artefacts have been locked in a chest and the keys are held by four members of the Braga community.

Left: Hermitage above Manang
Above: Himalayan Rescue Association at Manang, looking north
Right: Ruined fortress between Braga and Manang, looking south-east

138

The wind picks up in Manang, the prayer flags on the roof quiver, smoke curling from rooftops. The village awakens, resembling a Wild West frontier town with its flat-roofed and stone-walled buildings, each one a mini-fortress. Wild-looking characters on ponies canter by.

Left: Pony racing, Manang
Above: Souvenir stall, Manang

"How much money you paid in Norway?" Dipak asks, mentally trying to figure out where I fit into a different class scheme, measured by material wealth. I take an arbitrarily low figure, of 100 dollars a day, and convert it into rupees. "Five thousand rupees."

"Fibe tousand rupees! Every day?" he asks incredulously. I realize I have made a mistake. "You are reech."

141

There is a medieval atmosphere in the dark main room, with its low wooden rafters and stone slab floor. Shadowy images sitting hunched over tables are revealed by the light coming through a hole in the roof.

One sign of altitude sickness is irritation, and the only ones up here not exhibiting signs of irritation are the Nepalese staff who have more reason than anyone to be irritated.

The two boys and a girl collapse against a wall suffering headaches and signs of altitude sickness.

Left: Teahouse, Gunsang
Above: Shop boy, Manang
Right: Thorong Phedi, looking north-west towards the pass

"This my?" She points at my pencil. "No, this my," I reply.

She giggles. "This my?" She grabs my notebook. "This?"

Her tiny sister repeats, learning the tricks of the trade.

It is a beautiful day outside as we begin our climb. We are

determined to take our time and enjoy ourselves and take the

whole day "to go over the top".

Left: Making friends with a young girl backlit by early morning sun, Pisang
Right: Looking north-west towards Thorong La, Upper Thorong Phedi in background

A cairn beside the path is a poignant reminder of the dangers of high altitude: "Richard James Allan, Age 27, Died 24 February 1991 of AMS. Trekkers Beware".

Above: En route to Thorong La, looking nort-west
Right: The steep ascent from Thorong Phedi, looking south; the Annapurnas in the background

A fresh layer of snow covers the ground. Gossamer clouds against a cobalt-blue backdrop float dizzily about. The mountainsides appear less threatening, the heavy snowfall having filled the aggressive columns and crevices and covered the jagged rock outcrops.

I must use sunglasses to gaze across the open desert-like valley, at the Annapurnas, their sides blindingly silver-white. Snow blows off the crest of Annapurna II like smoke. Massive clumps of snow and ice cling to the almost vertical north face, leaving ugly overhangs suspended dangerously. The peaks and ridges, fluted columns of ice and snow, are another world, totally removed from this one.

En route to Thorong La; last view of Annapurnas II, III and IV, looking south

149

The valley, carved by a glacier, sports textbook lateral moraine lines on its sides. An oddly shaped waterfall hangs frozen. Further up the valley, to the north, vertical mountain faces disguise the fact that there is any possibility of climbing out of this apparent dead end.

En route to Thorong La, looking east towards Chulu

150

There are no trees, just a moonscape of rocks, like a desert, covered in a layer of snow. It is cold, but the effort of walking up the steep path soon has us wet with perspiration. We are surrounded by impossibly huge mounds of glacier moraine. Remnants of glaciers hang suspended from the rock face, massive overhangs waiting to crash down into the pass.

En route to Thorong La, looking east

After several false passes, the summit of Thorong La at 5,400 m/17,715 ft above sea level appears unexpectedly and anticlimactically.

We huddle around a fire at a makeshift teahouse in a derelict herders' hut.

Left: Approaching the summit of Thorong La, looking north-west
Above: Hut at the top of Thorong La

153

Descending from the path to the holy site of Muktinath is an anti-climax; it was not meant to be approached from above. Muktinath itself is the holy temple grounds, enclosed within a stone wall, where it is forbidden to stay.

Above left: Descending from Thorong La
towards Muktinath, looking south-west
Above right: Tibetan refugee
Right: Girl, Jagat

Long known as unruly rebels and bandits from the Kham province of Tibet, the Khampas were to become Tibet's last hope for freedom, as the tall and powerfully built warriors waged a rearguard action for many years against the occupying forces of the Chinese Communists. They were eventually forced to retreat to bases in Manang and Mustang.

She does not want us to go.

154

UPPER MUSTANG

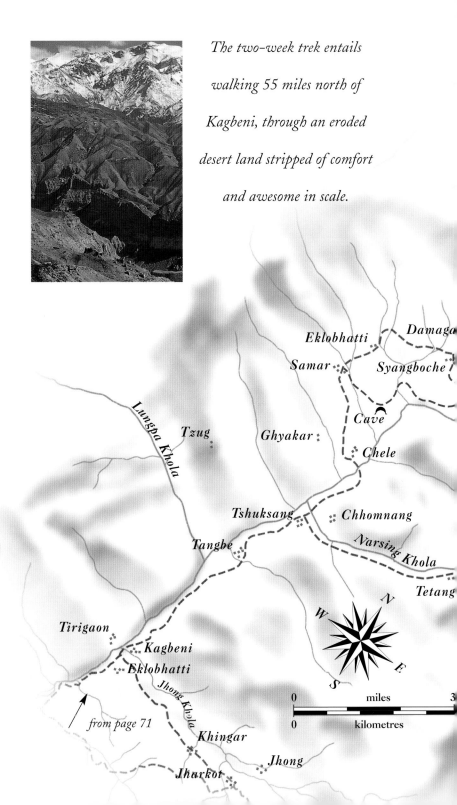

The two-week trek entails walking 55 miles north of Kagbeni, through an eroded desert land stripped of comfort and awesome in scale.

I had trekked in Nepal a dozen times and had long wanted to visit the hidden Kingdom of Upper Mustang, opened to foreign trekkers in 1992. To the inveterate traveller, Lomanthang is the equivalent of the Holy Grail, but the only way to visit this restricted area of Nepal is to pay for the privilege by taking the mandatory organized "group" tour with an accompanying government liaison officer.

The two-week trek entails walking 100 km/55 miles north of Kagbeni, through an eroded, brooding desert land stripped of comfort and awesome in scale, to Lomanthang, the hidden walled city in Upper Mustang. Then you have to hike back out, camping in remote fortress-like medieval villages. At altitudes consistently between 3,000 to 4,000 m/10,000 to 14,000 ft, whether it is the spring or the fall trekking season, it is going to be cold.

Historically not much more than a distant rumour, by 1960 only a dozen Westerners had ever set sight on the ancient Kingdom of Upper Mustang. The area clamped up tight as tension between China and the United States worsened and the CIA began funding and training Tibetan refugees in this geographical anomaly of political history sticking like the proverbial sore thumb into the gut of China's Tibet.

The history of Upper Mustang is based more on legend than written records, but from 1380 it became an independent kingdom under the rule of Amepal. The present Raja of Lo can trace his roots directly back twenty-five generations to the founder king of Lomanthang.

Leaving behind the relatively luxurious budget-conscious backpacker world of the Annapurna Circuit in Lower Mustang, you set out into one of the most isolated corners of the planet. The

156

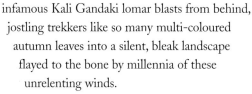

Namgya Gompa

Lomanthang (Mustang)

Lo Gekar

Marang

Ghami   Drakmar   Tsarang

Dri

Surkhang

ling

Ghechang Khola

Charan

Ten

Mustang Khola

Tange

Tange Khola

infamous Kali Gandaki lomar blasts from behind, jostling trekkers like so many multi-coloured autumn leaves into a silent, bleak landscape flayed to the bone by millennia of these unrelenting winds.

Upper Mustang is geologically, ethnically, linguistically, religiously and logistically all but Tibetan. A lucky quirk in Upper Mustang's history a couple of hundred years ago veered the Raja towards a feudal allegiance with the Gorkha kings to the south and eventually to the political sphere of modern Nepal, rather than Tibet. Now, in Upper Mustang, it is possible to witness a more authentic "Tibetan" world than is possible in Chinese Tibet.

The first stop is Tangbe, a walled village with a labyrinth of alleys and passageways set amidst fields of buckwheat, barley and wheat, and apple orchards. Within hours of leaving Kagbeni, there is an intense feeling of isolation, as if you are on a remote planet.

The first five villages encountered in Upper Mustang are a culturally unified group of people more closely related to the Manangis than the Lobas. Chele village, perched on a ridge, overlooks where the broad, boulder-strewn Kali Gandaki disappears furtively behind an apparently impenetrable cliff into the claustrophobic confines of a hidden canyon. Suffering the inevitable headache inspired by flying up to high altitude, and walking even higher, we set camp on the edge of Chele. After a perfunctory curry dinner in the bowels of a house formed of rammed mud, we beat a hasty retreat through a swirling snowstorm, and crept into the buffeted walls of our tent.

The ancient trade route diverts from the riverbed and climbs along a pathway cut high into the cliff face, before once again egressing into a sweeping, battered landscape. For the next five days as the dusting of fresh snow melted, we were lashed north into the austere land of Lo, through a succession of ominous fortress villages where icy mountain streams are manoeuvred through carefully constructed aqueducts, artificial brooks filling turquoise ponds feeding bone-dry terraces. Haunting in its stark immensity, the scenic equivalent of walking up the Grand Canyon, but with the added bonus of the Himalayan backdrop, this trail, several thousand years old, threads innumerable stupas, chortens, kanis, gompas and mani walls liberally washed in natural clay pigments of ochre, yellow and blue-grey. Resembling extensions to the man-made structures, multi-coloured sedimentary cliffs tower thousands of feet high, riddled with inter-connecting caves housing forgotten troglodytes whose origins are lost to antiquity. On almost every strategic hilltop you pass below the mute, crumbling ruins of forts. Whoever dominated Mustang controlled this unique corridor through the Himalayas, and thus the lucrative trade between the highlands of Central Asia and the tropical plains of India. Taxes levied on yak caravans carrying rock salt from the Tibetan Plateau south, and mule trains weaving north from the lowlands, guaranteed a prosperity that the skeletal mud fortresses and villages belie.

From cairns and poles at every pass, prayer flags snap with such velocity in the gale-force currents of air that it is easy to mistake their distant din for engines, but there are no vehicles here, not even a man-powered bicycle or cart wheel. Sharing the path in both directions march heavily laden donkeys, mules, ponies, dzo and yaks, driven along by whistling, wild-eyed men with braided hair wrapped in topknots and Mongolian features burnt brown by the sun and beaten by the wind. Most of these tough characters are blissfully drunk, a customary stratagem in dealing with the daily harshness of life here.

We ate our meals with everyone else, in the murky kitchens of the fortress-like homes. Despite a protective perimeter wall of firewood and frail kindling on the roofs of the houses where we camped, the afternoon breeze pummelled the tent like a loose sail in a gale. Temperatures were low enough that our water bottles inside the tent were frozen by morning.

With less than a thousand visitors making this trek into Upper Mustang annually since 1992, the villages and the people are remarkably untainted by the trappings of the modern Western world. Through an eroded, melancholy landscape you reach Lomanthang, the most important fortress community of them all, nestled on a rugged empty plain against a backdrop of extravagant wild spaces extending into Tibet.

At the only gates of the walled capital comprising some 150 fortress-like houses and four gompas, a gauntlet of pleading children perched on steps below a gigantic prayer wheel assailed us for rupees. Being early March, the Raja was out, sensibly wintering in Kathmandu, and in his place two formidable Tibetan mastiffs prowled about, their impressive snarls reverberating within the thick walls of his five-storeyed mud castle. Guarding the entrance to the home of the Raja's nephew, where we camped, are less threatening ram and dog skulls encased within a spider's web of coloured string to entangle harmful demons attempting to enter the house.

The photographs taken by Michel Peissel in 1964 in his classic book *Mustang: A Lost Tibetan Kingdom* portray perfectly the scenes in each of the villages, although it is now almost four decades later.

Returning via a higher route, even more magnificent than the walk up, the snowy backdrop of the distant Himalayas is a constant reminder of how far it is to Jomsom. For the next few days we returned down steep-sided ravines and implausible gorges, over exposed passes encompassing stunning views of the rolling, snow-covered peaks of the Tibetan Plateau, camping in the shadow of gompas where lamas have secluded themselves in solitary confinement for three years, three months, and three days.

Descending from Ghara Gompa, Lo's monochromatic sepia-browns become stained vibrant blood-red, bruised-blue and green, funereal grey-black, in the fantastic pinnacles and precipices flanking Drakmar down to Ghami. We diverted off the wide path into a shadowy portal, a lean chasm thousands of feet deep, to Rangbyung, a cave tucked high in the cliff face where a Tibetan refugee lama endures the frigid winter to reside there throughout the year, keeping company a host of Buddhas reputed to sprout out of stalagmites and rock.

En route from Tangbe to Kagbeni with Nilgiri behind, looking south

The closer we got to the Himalayas, and Jomsom, the more the winds seemed determined to hammer us back to Lomanthang. Here the currents of air thrash north consistently at 40 kph/25 mph, with sustained gusts of up to 120 kph/65 mph an hour; any exposed flesh was effectively sandblasted, as the winds hurled the detritus scoured from the bed of the Kali Gandaki into our faces.

Reaching the backpackers' world at blustery Jomsom, where we would be catapulted early the following morning with relative ease in a Twin Otter back to Pokhara, we abandoned the exclusivity of our entourage of staff and shunning our tent found ourselves a popular lodge, miraculously equipped with a real bath and solar-heated hot water.

In our newly achieved opulence, I awaited my turn and opened a bag of salted nuts, then refilled the tub with scalding water, and immersed myself to my chin for two hours, savouring a bottle of wine and the cashews while waxing lyrical about our journey, which somehow kept my wife giggling. "What was the most memorable part of the trip?" I shouted through the bathroom door.

The swaddle of blankets muffled her reply. "When you gave the nice lama living in the cave your red down jacket and sleeping bag." I near froze for two days after that spontaneous act of generosity, but it was worth it to enhance my long-term karma and guarantee a better reincarnation in the next life. "What was your most memorable moment?" she asked.

Forgetting the stunning landscape we had been privileged to observe, I raised the refilled glass of Bordeaux and, wiggling my grimy wrinkled toes through the surface of steaming scum, answered only half-facetiously, "This."

Looking north across the Kali Gandaki towards Tangbe

When the US stopped its military support to the Khampas in 1971, the guerillas naturally enough continued to fight. The Chinese government complained bitterly about the Khampa bases in Mustang. Eventually most of the Khampa guerillas realized that it was pointless to continue without support from the US and without the tacit approval from Nepal in allowing them to base their operations in Mustang.

How much easier to feel at peace in the awesome nature and simple lifestyle of these mountains and people, far away from the daily demands and pressure of our own high-speed, high-tech, stressful and materialistic Western lives.

Above: Playing Tigers and Goats, drawn in the dust instead of using a board, with different sized pebbles representing four tigers and twenty goats
Right: Chele

Areas in shadow are white with the frost covering the rocks. Often the path is so narrow and tortuous and the drop precipitous.

In this lofty place it is easy to read significance into the more commonplace experiences.

Even here in this remote village, the cooking fire is no longer the traditional open hearth.

Left: Between Chele and Samar
Above: An act of kindness in Rangbyung holy cave
Right: Teahouse, Damagaon

As I stand on the ramparts of the old

fortress, my shadow is cast long,

descending to the fields below.

The area north is still a restricted area.

There are various reasons for this, but

sensitivity to the Chinese/Tibetan border

is paramount.

Left and right: Geling, looking north

Soon the sunlight hits us. It is not warm, at least not immediately, but psychologically it makes a difference to see the ground around reflecting the warm light.

Unlike other areas of the country, Mustang pays no land tax to Nepal. It is, in effect, an independent principality.

Above: An essential irrigation pond overlooking Geling, looking north towards an abandoned fortress
Right: Remnants of a fortress, and gompa and chortens in Geling, looking east

168

Next to him is a heavy-set, tough-looking man, with square shoulders, and a face that could be native American. From his left ear hang large chunks of pink coral and turquoise. His braided hair reaches down his back. We are served Tibetan tea, a savoury drink combined with salt and yak butter.

The thought occurs to me: the major reason for the simplicity and even the attractiveness of life here is the exclusion of vehicles of any kind.

Left above: Raja's family home, Ghami
Left below: Ghami, looking west
Above: Mani wall between Ghami and Tsarang,
looking north

At another long mani wall images of Tara with ripe breasts, and images of Tantric sex

and esoteric yantras honouring the deities, tantalize ignorant passers-by like myself.

Mummified yak skulls stare sightlessly out from a cavity below the effigies.

171

In the distance a canyon of fluted
organ pipes lies astride the riverbed,
stained red in the saturated colours
of the evening light. I am living a
dream come true. I am exactly
where I want to be. The way is the
goal, there is no target.

At the top of a ridge I pick up a
stone and place it on the cairn,
which grows higher as each traveller
who chooses to do so makes a
contribution in thanks to the gods of
lonely windswept crossings.

Left: Drakmar, looking north
Right: Chorten at southern entrance to Tsarang,
looking north

But most dramatic of all, the village is entirely enclosed by high solid walls, with few windows facing the outside.

The present Raja of Lo can trace his roots directly back twenty-five generations to the founder king of Lomanthang.

The status of Mustang today is unique in Nepal. A token amount of tax is paid by the King of Mustang, but he is allowed in return to collect any amount of taxes and money from his people and to dispose of this sum.

Left: Gompa and ruined castle, Tsarang
Above: Raja's family home, Ghami
Right: Giving out grain to villagers at the Raja's family home, Tsarang

I want to get back into that desert–like primitive world where it is so easy to imagine oneself taken back 500 years.

Mustang is a geographic anomaly, sticking into Tibet like a sore thumb as far as the Chinese are concerned. Although linked to Tibet geographically, ethnically and politically, the Kingdom of Mustang during the late eighteenth century became politically indebted to the Raja of Jumla to the south.

Above: Mule train heading north between Drakmar
and Ghami
Right: Boy lama at Raja's family home, Tsarang,
looking east

Behind us the vertical rock face is

pock-marked with hundreds of caves.

Fortresses lie below us and up the valley.

Early morning light illuminates the

spectacular landscape with a warmth and

clarity that will be idelibly etched in my

memory. I have rarely felt more sated.

The air is palpably fresh and clean, the

sky immaculate and immense.

Left: Looking south towards Tsarang
Right: Looking south-east up at the ruined fortress
dominating the approach to Tsarang from the north

The villages are similar to Kagbeni, but in better condition. The red gompa is taller, perhaps four storeys high. The mud-packed dzong looks to be in better shape, higher and bigger than those in the Dzong Valley.

The rolling plateaux and hills to the north are Tibet.

Left: Gompa, Tsarang
Right: Looking south-east towards Tsarang

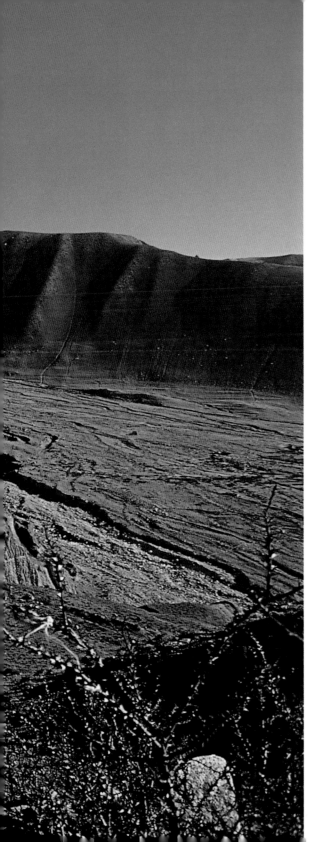

The pony has a peculiar gait, with small, quick, dainty steps, which makes it impossible to post while trotting.

Above: Lo Gekar, looking north-east
Left: En route to Lo Gekar to Ghami, looking north towards high pass leading to Lomanthang

Cairns topped with prayer flags line each hump of every ridge. In this high-altitude environment everything seems to have spiritual connotations, and it does not surprise me that Tibetan historical literature was almost exclusively religious in context.

She asks for the kerchief that is wrapped around my neck. "No is possible," I tell her. It has sentimental value for me. "Everything possible," she replies coyly. She is right; everything does seem possible up here. And to prove the point, I symbolically unknot the memory and give it to her.

An old man, fingering well-worn prayer beads, mumbles "Om Mani Padme Hum".

Above and left: Main entrance to Lomanthang, north-facing wall

Over doorways, goat skulls covered in cloth and a backdrop of crossed sticks and a spider's web of coloured threads ward off evil spirits. The white threads of the zor are for the gods. The coloured threads are for the tsen, the evil spirits which lie in wait everywhere, ready to do harm.

When I entered the gompa I was anxious to do the right thing. I did not want to offend. Now I realize there was no danger of that. Some women gossip; others pray; the young lama chats and laughs with a woman in front. The other lamas drink tea during the recitation of prayers.

Left: Raja's fortress, Lomanthang
Below: Interior of community hall in gompa, Lomanthang

The air is dry, like a desert, but

considerably warmer than the other side

of the Thorong La towards Manang.

Snow lies only on the north-facing slopes,

protected from the glare of the sun. To the

south, east and west snow-plastered

Himals and the Just Hills pierce the sky;

to the north sprawls the immense

Tibetan plateau.

Gompa at Namgya, looking south-west

NOTE ON THE PHOTOGRAPHY

All of the photographs were taken with Nikon cameras. Many were taken with a second-hand Nikon bought in Kathmandu with a 28mm and telephoto lens. This camera worked well, but most of the more recent shots were taken with a Nikon F4 or F5, one with a 20mm and the other with a 35–210mm Nikon lens, also bought in Kathmandu. The F4 and F5 bodies are particularly good at keeping out high levels of dust. Unfortunately, slung around the neck, they feel like millstones. I am particularly fond of the 20mm lens because it has great depth and wide range of field so that it can tell a detailed comprehensive story far better than a closely cropped telephoto image. I use a polarizer lens to get rid of the extraneous light which tends to deepen colours, especially the naturally cobalt blue Himalayan sky which can sometimes look too cobalt blue. Film was Kodak slide film: Kodachrome 64 or Kodak Elite Chrome 100, also bought and developed in Kathmandu.

I am entirely self-taught as a photographer. What I look for in a photograph is primarily light, and composition. I rarely take photographs after nine in the morning, or before four in the afternoon, because of the harshness of the light and the propensity for high contrasts between sunlit areas and shadow, landscape or portrait. I rarely use a flash indoors. I improvize, using an aluminium lid, or even the pot itself, to reflect rays of light. I usually have the camera set on automatic which allows the Nikon's F4 and F5 technology to deal with the light and focus, giving me the chance to concentrate on the composition. Many of my images are taken spontaneously without much premeditation and without benefit of a tripod. Nevertheless, I establish a friendly relationship with anyone I take a photograph of, and ask permission first. Most locals are happy to be photographed, although some want a copy sent to them, and others ask for money. If asked, I try to do both. Often older people with characterful faces are embarrassed because they feel they are old and don't want their image taken. While most residents of the Annapurnas are amenable to being photographed, the Loba in Upper Mustang were reluctant subjects.

Few of these images were taken during my first trip around the Annapurna Circuit when I wrote my travelogue, *Annapurna Circuit: Himalayan Journey*. I find it difficult to focus on the writing of a travelogue and the taking of photographs beyond the most conventional of snapshots. In many ways, writing and photography are mutually exclusive activities. Photography is all about light and composition, while writing is about all the senses: smells, taste, sounds, feelings, thoughts, mood and ambience. As a photographer I'm up before dawn and still wandering around at sunset, scrambling around and waiting, usually alone, for that magical subdued light to illuminate mountains or people. By contrast, as a writer, I'm sitting in the kitchen with the owner, or in the dining room with other foreigners inside a bhatti, actively involved, listening to stories and participating in conversations, communicating with locals and trekkers alike.

Gompa, Lo Gekar, looking north